#GoPongo

#GoPongo

Launching: The World's Largest
Communications Network
Connecting Every Device for
Every Person in Every Language
Everywhere on Earth

Daniel Webster

Daniel Webster

CONTENTS

CONTENTS

This book is dedicated to my parents,
Bud and Charlotte Webster.
Thank you for allowing me to dream big
and giving me permission to believe that having big dreams was normal.

#GoPongo: Launching the World's Largest Communications Network Connecting Every Device for Every Person in Every Language Everywhere on Earth

By Daniel Webster

Copyright 1996, 1998, 1999, 2009, 2010, 2014, 2018, 2019, 2020, 2021 by Daniel Webster

Published By Daniel Webster *daniel@dwebserve.com*

This book is specifically created as an invitation to: Dr. John Chesnut, Wycliffe Bible Translators and **Tim Neu**, Wycliffe Associates; **Rupert Murdoch**, News Corp and Fox Corporation; **Hans Vestberg**, Verizon Communications; **Larry Ellison**, Oracle Corporation; **Robert Mark Bakish**, ViacomCBS; **Elon Musk**, SpaceX and Tesla, Inc.; **James D. Farley Jr.**, Ford Motor Company; **David Scott Taylor**, Procter & Gamble; **William Rodney McMullen**, Kroger; **Sir Tim Berners-Lee**, Inrupt; **@Jack Dorsey**, Twitter; **Robert A. Kotick**, Activision Blizzard; **Roger Goodell**, National Football League; **Dr. Patrick Soon-Shiong**, Los Angeles Times and Nant Capital; **David D. Smith**, Sinclair Broadcast Group; **Charles "Charlie" C. Hale**, Hale Global and Patch; **John DeCero**, Mechanics Bank; **Michael Hallén**, Vizrt Group and NewTek; plus, three companies yet to be determined.

In this book, "Smoogle-Boogle" is Google, "TubeyTV" is YouTube TV, "Bluebookey-Facey Thing" is Facebook, "GramItInAnInstant" is Instagram, "Quibyebye" is Quibi, "Rainforest" is Amazon, "Bic-TheNet" is Netflix, "Fruit" is Apple, "MartInWalls" is Walmart and "PannettFannett" is Gannett.

Preface: Pongo in Abstract

1. **Problem:** There is no digital solution for a successful local news service. If there was, thousands of local newspapers would not close down. They would change over to the digital solution and continue to operate.

   Solution: Build a digital complete system which allows a local news service to successfully operate, making enough revenue to continue to deliver local news to a local community at a profit. Saving the free press and community news organizations will also save the internet.

2. **Problem:** Current monetization formulas and platforms are focused on a massive number of viewers to create a revenue stream to support an individual's work product, such as local news.

   Solution: Create a formula and platform which allows a local news content creator to make a living from support of a population of 6,000 to 7,000.

3. **Problem:** Various income streams from a local newspaper print edition business formula are not available online.

   Solution: Create a platform which harvests revenue from the various income streams which are needed to fund a local news operation.

4. **Problem:** The previous print edition business model harvested revenue from large national advertisers and small town local ads.

   Solution: A digital internet successful local news solution must take advantage of national co-op advertising and local business ads.

5. **Problem:** Many large major news brands have struggled and closed due to a lack of revenue to support their large news efforts.
Solution: Create a platform which gives a major national news outlet the additional revenue stream to survive, by allowing a major brand to receive revenue from small local advertising sources.

6. **Problem:** News services cannot survive financially by online advertising and subscriptions alone. The model has yet to succeed although countless efforts have been made.
Solution: News outlets and other content creators must create a commission structure or mechanism representing actual sales of goods and services sold/consumed.

7. **Problem:** There is no current solution for content creators to make commissions and royalties from selling goods and services created by national or local manufacturers and providers.
Solution: Create a solution for consumers to purchase goods or services online, also pay a commission and royalty to a content creator when the sale happens as a result of the consumer viewed content, advertisement which sold them on the product or service.

8. **Problem:** Building commission-based digital service platforms are cost prohibitive for small news outlets. The expense would not allow cost recovery in markets with a customer base of 6,000 to 7,000 consumers.
Solution: Build the platform on a large scale, so small local content creators can use the system.

9. **Problem:** The digital coding for all of the various pieces and parts to create the platform has already been created by different large corporations.
Solution: Merge corporate coding assets into a single platform.

10. **Problem:** Large corporations require a financial incentive to increase shareholders value.

Solution: Design a financial formula to acquire existing corporate digital coding.

11. **Problem:** The large corporations which own the digital coding to create the solution must be legally protected from the content, goods and services flowing through their coding.

    Solution: Create a legal corporate structure which removes the liability of the content, goods and services from the corporations which own the digital code.

12. **Problem:** The ultimate solution for financially saving small town news, is needed by other content providers, such as online education, internet radio, online influencers, political campaigns, religious institutions, to name a few.

    Solution: The platform created for news also can be used for other content. Broaden the scope of the platform to apply to all digital communications. Highly monetize all content.

13. **Problem:** Content goes global on the internet and the financial solution must be able to work everywhere in the world.

    Solution: Make the platform work in one country with a simple interactive shell which can easily translate into other languages and monetary systems.

14. **Problem:** For this platform to work financially, nearly every moment within the system must be monetized. Users will not favor a highly monetized system which obviously is making money off them constantly. Also, they will prefer a system that does not monetize their private information.

    Solution: . Pay a user to make money from doing what they already are willing to do for free. Create a platform which makes people happy to be monetized because they benefit too, through potential income and maintaining privacy.

15. **Problem:** This platform requires a paid contract with everyone involved.

    Solution: Make a platform which charges a small amount everyone can afford just to get them into a paid contract for service.

16. **Problem:** Once a product, service or content leaves the network, it loses its legal protection of the platform's paid contract.
    Solution: Make the platform able to handle the entire process, start to finish, big to small.
17. **Problem:** The coding has already been created by approximately 21 of the largest corporations in the world.
    Solution: Provide financial incentive to bring those 21 corporations together. The creator of Pongo believes your company is one of those 21 corporations.
18. **Problem:** Competing platforms have billions of dollars to spend building out their own solution using many of the concepts from the Pongo formula.
    Solution: Create a method for all platforms, websites, apps and users to plug and play into Pongo at a nominal cost structure. The superior revenue power of Pongo will attract other businesses once they recognize that they can also generate previously captured revenue.
19. **Problem:** None of this fits in the current corporate paradigm.

Solution: Smash the old paradigm using a new model -- Pongo.

By creating the above solution, we have just created what has the potential to become The World's Largest Communications Network Connecting Every Device for Every Person in Every Language Everywhere on Earth.

Daniel Webster
Pongo's Parent

1

Newspaper 'No Man's Land'

" WHEN I CLOSED MY PIONEER PRESS, $300,000 IN REVENUE "
CONTINUED TO SIT ON THE TABLE. IT'S STILL WAITING TO BE
PICKED UP. TAKEN TOGETHER, BILLIONS OF DOLLARS ARE STILL
ON THE TABLE WAITING TO BE SPENT IN THE LOCAL NEWS
MARKETS WHICH LOST THEIR NEWS SOURCES. THAT CASH
DIDN'T GO TO OUR LARGE TECH FIRMS. I KNOW.

When I bought my hometown small newspaper, the former Editor and Publisher Gary Mortenson gave me a piece of strange advice.

"There's a 'no man's land' in the newspaper business. Between $150,000 and $300,000 in revenue, a newspaper can't turn a profit. You can't make any money," Gary explained. "You either need to keep it small, so you can run it basically as a one-person operation, or you will have to get over $300,000 to become large enough to make a profit. Your expenses will eat you up in no man's land."

Such advice seemed like nonsense to me at the time. Gary was correct.

Gary had kept his news operation small. I chose to push and beef it up.

I proved Gary right nearly every year I published the Pioneer Press in my small town.

Year after year, I hovered around $300,000 in gross revenue. It was nearly impossible to turn a decent profit. My biggest expenses, printing, distribution and payroll, ate it all up.

For a small hyperlocal market such as mine, $300,000 was the maximum amount in revenue I could bring in.

I tried every trick in the book to make my newspaper a financial success. I attempted the news conglomerate approach. I bought the struggling, court adjudicated Butte Valley Star, founded in 1929, for $1. I purchased the Klamath Courier, in the Klamath Falls Basin, for the equivalent of a sack of potatoes -- literally running my eastern news editions out of a potato warehouse in Malin, Ore. Even my regional approach to news couldn't pay off.

I went into the news business in the wrong era, as local news was dying.

The notion of going digital was enticing. It would eliminate my two greatest expenses of printing and distribution. My revenue, however, would tank.

Going digital wasn't a solution. I would take my revenue from $300,000 to mere peanuts, with the digital revenue solutions.

Nearly all of the $300,000 in revenue would remain on the table, unable to be picked up, in a digital solution. Going digital wasn't actually a solution.

I wasn't alone.

According to a report from University of North Carolina Hussman School of Media and Journalism, since 2004, we have lost one-fourth -- 2,100 -- of our newspapers in the United States, including 70 dailies and more than 2,000 weeklies or nondailies.

At the end of 2019, the United States had 6,700 newspapers, fallen from almost 9,000 in 2004, UNC Hussman reports.

If there was a viable digital solution, local news wouldn't die. An online solution would allow local news to thrive, turning a profit from the internet.

Ultimately, I had to shut down my newspaper and become a statistic. The shame was that I had the solution.

When I closed my Pioneer Press, $300,000 in revenue continued to sit on the table. It's still waiting to be picked up. Taken together, billions of dollars are still sitting on the table waiting to be spent in the local news markets which lost their news sources. That cash didn't go to our large tech firms. I know. I see who is advertising on my social media and streaming feeds. My former advertisers aren't spending the money they previously gave me.

We didn't have to do it this way.

There's a solution.

The solution works for far more than local news. It works for major news brands, social media influencers, movie studios, sports enterprises, political campaigns, product manufacturers, service providers and more. The solution is all encompassing. The solution to save local news has the ability to save the internet.

The solution is super-simple and easy to build. We've already created all the pieces and parts. We just need to sew the various pieces and parts into one complete platform.

The solution to the problem is a talking dog named Pongo.

This book, #GoPongo, is my request for you to help me launch Pongo, by throwing Pongo a bone.

2

The Secret Concert in the Hungarian Forest

" I BELIEVE IN THE CORE OF MY HEART, IF WE FOLLOW THIS "
FOUNDATIONAL PRINCIPLE TO BUILD MY NETWORK, PONGO
WILL BE THE NEXT GUTENBERG PRESS -- AND THIS TIME, IT'S
DIGITAL AND PERSONAL. WHEN HISTORY IS WRITTEN SO FAR,
WE WILL READ OF THE TWO MONUMENTAL INVENTIONS WHICH
RADICALLY ALTERED THE WORLD'S COMMUNICATIONS: THE
GUTENBERG PRESS AND PONGO.

In 1982 and 1983 I traveled with the Continental Singers and Orchestra behind the Iron Curtain to bring my faith's Holy Scripture to a world through song where a ruling government reigned supreme under the influence of the former Soviet Union at the time.

Some of the countries where we performed do not exist today -- the map has changed.

Through most of our tour, we had agents following us everywhere we went, hiding in bushes with their machine guns watching every move we made.

There was one day, in Hungary, we got on the bus and the local man handling our concert schedule gave us directions to take a long, bumpy drive out to the middle of a forest, far from any town.

It took us more than an hour for our bus to arrive at our "concert location." We pulled into a clearing in the forest, which made no sense at all. We were so far removed from any population, we joked that we would be singing to a bunch of trees.

Our normal routine of setting up lights and sound equipment went out the window. There was no electricity for miles.

There wasn't really a set time for this concert. It would start when the audience arrived. There were no billboards and posters plastered throughout towns and cities announcing our concert in the forest. We were told that the promotion was all word of mouth.

Agents obviously were not aware of our concert -- they weren't hiding in the bushes and behind trees this time. It was a secret concert.

As we hung out waiting, from the forest, through the trees, people began to walk out into the clearing. More people began to show up. They appeared from the trees encircling us.

Considering it took us an hour to slowly drive on the rough, dirt road through the forest, the people walking had to walk hours to get there.

Thousands upon thousands had made their way to the clearing in the middle of the forest. Our interpreter said it was time to start.

We were trained to sing with softer blended voices, allowing the sound system to amplify our singing and instruments.

Seeing the size of the audience, without amplification, our director instructed us to all sing in the loudest full voice possible, our orchestra was to blast their instruments like never before, in order to reach the masses.

As we sang, more and more people continued to arrive.

When we finished our concert, the audience wouldn't let us leave. They chanted and screamed for more. We gave an encore. They wanted more. We gave them another encore. They still wanted more.

Obviously, they hadn't walked for hours, just to hear an hour and a half concert.

Our interpreter told us to do the entire concert again.

We started at the top and performed the entire show.

More. They wanted more.

We gave them the whole concert a third time.

We were aware that it was now approaching darkness and the audience would have to walk through the night to get home.

After the concert, two young Hungarian men in their 20s came up to visit with me. They spoke English fairly well.

As we talked, they told me about their secret church where they met every week. When they got together, they exchanged their Bible pages. That wasn't a concept that made sense.

I asked them to explain.

They both pulled out from their hidden spot in their clothes a folded, printed page in the Hungarian language, which appeared to be a page from the Bible. They showed it to me. It still didn't make sense.

They explained, their whole community shared a single Bible. It's all they had. Bibles were illegal. They carefully ripped out every page and gave everyone a page of their Holy Scripture for the week. The most exciting part of getting together every week was receiving their new page of the Bible. This too wasn't a concept that made sense.

"You only have one Bible?"

"One," as he held up a finger.

"Can you get another Bible?" I asked.

"No. Never."

"Hold on a moment. Stay right here. Don't move," I told them.

I ran to the bus, opened my carry on bag. I grabbed my compact, smartphone-size full Bible I had purchased for the trip, because it was lightweight.

I ran back to the two boys and handed it to them.

"Here, I can get another."

One held it, silently, felt it, turned it, didn't open it. The other watched intensely.

"I've never held a Bible before," he said.

It wasn't a concept that made sense to me.

He handed it to his friend. "Here. Hold it."

They started sobbing.

I had no understanding for the context of their visceral emotional response. It was one of the most impactful scenes I've ever experienced in my lifetime.

In their tears, they handed it back to me.

"Thank you for letting us hold your Bible."

"No. It's yours. My gift. I can get another one when I get back to America," I replied.

I'm a print guy. I love print. One of my favorite books is the massive hardbound most important front pages of the Los Angeles Times. I could flip through it for hours, all over again.

In my view, the Gutenberg Press was the greatest invention of all time.

Publishing the Holy Scripture for EVERY religion, culture, country, language, language group, tongue, tribe is the highest calling for a printing press.

It also is the foundation of all free communications. Publishing the Holy Scripture for every religion opens the floodgates for all other freedoms. Making sure all Holy Scripture in every religion is translated into every language for every person everywhere on earth establishes freedom of speech, allowing all other freedoms to flow.

Johannes Gutenberg only had one audience, one community, one language and one religion in his target market when he used his new printing press to completely alter the world of communications. Imagine targeting all languages, all religions, all communities, all audiences, all people, everywhere in the world. Pongo will do just that.

I believe in the core of my heart, if we follow this foundational principle to build this network, Pongo will be the next Gutenberg Press -- and this time, it's digital and personal.

When history is written so far, we will read of the two monumental inventions which radically altered the world's communications: the Gutenberg Press and Pongo.

Which is why I am inviting Wycliffe Bible Translators to be in my number one spot in the Founding 21 Pongo Launch Engine. They are the world's foremost translators. It is a solid foundation for our mission statement that will have a translation system by which all Holy Scriptures -- and all communications -- are able to reach every person in every language everywhere on earth -- from the biggest to the smallest.

Wycliffe Bible Translators has translated enough of the Bible into 3,415 languages to use artificial intelligence applied to its Bible translations to place the Pongo Engine core public interaction shell into those languages. A digital recording of a native person reading their Holy Scripture in their native tongue could be used by artificial intelligence (AI) to allow Pongo to speak in those native tongues.

I believe that AI applied to someone digitally and verbally reading in that person's native tongue would allow an AI talking dog to speak. Pongo must ultimately speak every language.

Wycliffe is the most advanced in general translation work around the world. By Wycliffe being one of the 21 Pongo Launch Engine companies, Pongo conceivably, shortly after launching, could be in as many as 3,415 language groups. Although, Pongo will likely launch in one language, English, it will automatically transform into speaking all languages possible.

According to Wycliffe, 3,945 languages still have no Scripture completed, with 2,014 languages still in need of translation work to begin. Pongo has some work to do. Our job won't be finished anytime soon, although I believe AI will be used to push that process along.

Smoogle-Boogle is currently translating 108 languages. Bluebookey-Facey Thing is now up to 100.

Someday, as I travel the world, everywhere I go, I want to meet people who thank me for bringing their Holy Scripture for their religion in their language directly to them. They won't be sobbing, because it will seem natural and normal at that time. Pongo will have changed the world.

Pongo is bigger than any tech company ever built. It goes back to our mission statement. We are to build the world's largest communications network connecting every device in every language for every person everywhere on earth. This has never been done before. We have nothing to compare it with. To comprehend the concepts we must set aside how we know tech company start-ups have been created previously.

The task is huge. How we do it is super-simple. It's all been created. We don't have to come up with anything new. We just need to have a quilting bee and eat some delicious pie. Quilts and pie, my friends, quilts and pie. You can't go wrong with quilts and pie.

3

How To Launch Pongo

" THE POWER AND POTENTIAL OF THE INTERNET HAS YET TO "
FULLY BE UNLEASHED IN A BUSINESS MODEL. PONGO IS
CHANGING THAT WITH THIS BOOK.

In the olden days, people would submit a business plan for consideration. Those days are over. We are living in a new era. Pongo can't be launched by submitting a business plan to 21 prospective corporate founders. It's a ludicrous notion for Pongo. There's no point in my going through the hassle and drama.

For Pongo to launch, I must bring together 21 of the biggest, most powerful companies and entities which have already created all of the pieces and parts to build Pongo.

I own and control the patent pending for the business systems and processes of the Pongo Engine. These proprietary systems and processes can only be accessed exclusively through a signed written agreement between myself, Daniel Webster, and the prospective 21 Pongo Founding Engine members.

To get the word out to the heads of these corporate families and entities, I created a series of videos on my Twitter account @danielwebster and wrote this book. You are likely reading this book because I sent you here from a video on Twitter. Thank you for purchasing my book.

To get attention, I must create buzz. I'm hoping #GoPongo trends. To help with that process, I went so far as to title this book with that hashtag.

I hope 100,000 people will download this book to get the word out. Will you help me by sharing and talking about this book on social media? Please help me make #GoPongo trend.

If @Jack Dorsey is a super-cool dude, maybe he'll throw Pongo a bone and force my #GoPongo to trend on Twitter. Oh, that's right, they don't do that.

There's actually nothing normal about Pongo. The concept has never been launched in the world. Nobody has come up with my formula to do it. It can't be constructed under our normal ways in the corporate world.

Which is why I'm using such an abnormal approach to launching this tech company.

I have put together a unique formula and corporate structure to accommodate the nuances of the Pongo plan.

Let's do some smashing and destruction first.

Big business folks are so proud of their little "paradigm shift" they do in corporate management. They go "ooooo and ahhhh" when they are presented with a paradigm shift moving a paradigm a few inches or a couple of feet.

Pongo isn't a paradigm shift. To understand and build Pongo, we must first take the various paradigms y'all are holding and throw them on the ground, smash them, stomp them, destroy them, break them all into tiny pieces and parts. Make sure the pieces and parts are no longer recognizable as the former paradigms.

Now, look down at the floor on all the broken pieces and parts.

We are going to pick up many of those pieces and parts and sew them back together in a different structure, as one new, complete, solid, cohesive digital internet engine. The new Engine we create from the pieces and parts is Pongo. Many of those pieces are found in the Verizon and

Oracle families of companies. These two corporations would make up the backbone.

As you see, none of the pieces and parts are new -- they've all been created already. We are just forming them into a new structure.

A good physical picture to give you an idea of how we build Pongo, is a quilt. Yes, Pongo is in essence a quilting project, taking various pieces of different fabric -- the technology coding -- from numerous fabric manufacturers and sewing all of the unique pieces of tech fabric into one gorgeous, complete singular quilt.

Such, building Pongo is akin to a massive corporate quilting bee.

I have the pattern and the formula to make the quilt. I need to bring all the fabric manufacturers -- technology companies -- together for my big Pongo quilting bee.

I have identified the 21 companies I believe have created the pieces and parts for our giant tech quilt. This book is my personal invitation for us all to come together and have our founding planning session to explore putting this all into one technology quilt.

Building Pongo is actually pretty easy. It shouldn't take long to build out -- maybe as fast as four to six months -- considering we've already created it all. We now have to sew pieces together.

This book and the accompanying videos are my "crowdsourcing" project to get everyone's attention, hopefully.

Unlike other crowdsourcing projects, I don't need cash from those in the crowd. I need your connections.

Therefore, if you know a person who is the head of one of the mentioned companies or know someone who knows the president and CEO, will you please do me a crowdsourcing favor and tip them off that I'm wanting to meet with them to discuss launching Pongo?

In this crowdsourcing invitation, otherwise called my #GoPongo book and video series, I will be specifically using the name of the entities I believe are the ones which should and could come together to launch Pongo.

If I refer to a funny name for a company, that is my indication that they are not on my list of 21.

For example, the National Football League is one of the 21 "technology" companies I want to be part of the founding Pongo engine, thus, I will refer to the NFL by name.

You notice that I consider the NFL to be a "technology" company? In this era, we are all now technology companies, just some tech companies play football. It's the nature of our world now.

The NFL is important to Pongo, as they will be building an engine to broadcast high school sports using an engine powerful enough to run the NFL.

If I call up NFL Commissioner Roger Goodell, I may get a "Daniel who?"

I'm willing to bet, however, in this unique crowdsourcing project, someone knows Roger and can tell him, "there's a guy named Daniel Webster trying to connect with you."

I don't need NFL cash, I need their technology, expertise, experience and customer awareness. If Pongo is powerful enough to run every digital device -- from the digital jumbotron to the audience's digital cell phones, from the digital cameras on the field to the digital stream out of the stadium -- in one dynamic interactive experience, we've just built an engine which can also broadcast an interactive live football game for both the NFL and my small-town high school football field.

BTW, why can't I choose which camera I want to watch during the NFL football game? Everything is digital from the cameras in the stadium to my smart TV, correct?

Conversely, Mark's Bluebooky-Facey Thing is not one of the 21 companies I am inviting to the Pongo founding, such that you won't read in my book or hear in my videos a reference to the actual name of Bluebooky-Facey Thing. I will make reference to his social media company, as an example. Once Pongo is launched, Mark will likely give Pongo $2 a month to use the Pongo engine to make more cash for his

Bluebookey-Facey Thing, because my formula and engine is far superior to anything Mark has dreamed. Yes, his shareholders will demand it.

On the flip side, I am inviting @Jack Dorsey from Twitter to join the founding of Pongo's engine. I want Twitter to help build the engine that is capable and big enough, with a successful formula, that gives Twitter greater earning potential. If that happens, @Jack may call up Mark when Pongo is built, to tell Mark that he's just built an engine that Mark could use to make more money for his Bluebookey-Facey Thing.

I'm not seeking @Jack's cash, I need pieces of the technology Twitter has created, and I want @Jack to be able to make previously untapped cash and make money generated from Mark when he brings Mark's Bluebookey-Facey Thing in as a $2 a month Pongo user.

Are you starting to see that we aren't making a "paradigm shift" when we build Pongo?

Are you starting to understand that Pongo isn't a normal corporate structure?

4

The Pongo Engine

"THE PONGO COMPANY, THUS, WON'T CREATE THE TECHNOLOGY " ITSELF. PONGO WILL LICENSE THE TECHNOLOGY. THE PONGO COMPANY SEWS THE SLICES OF THE PIE TOGETHER. PONGO HAS THE QUILTERS SEWING THE INDIVIDUAL PIECES OF FABRIC TOGETHER TO MAKE THE OVERALL QUILT, WHICH ACTUALLY IS A PIE.

Pongo's Engine is all the core technology which runs the Pongo system. Everything runs through the Pongo Engine. Pongo doesn't create the technology in the Engine. The technology of the Engine has already been created by the 21 families of companies which are in the Engine upon the network's launch.

This technology is all used under a licensing contract for the technology, in exchange for a royalty payment based on the gross revenue running through the Engine. Each founding company receives an equal 1/21 share of the Engine's portion of the royalty pie.

The Founding 21 will also identify, based on their intimate knowledge of their particular businesses, what additional technologies need to be brought in to allow a full start to finish, big to small complete Pongo Engine.

The Founding 21 are chosen, not solely based on their technology and coding, but also their industry clout, unique perspectives, history and abilities to drive Pongo's launch. Further additional companies added to the Engine will be based primarily on the technology and coding they are adding in relation to the current Engine as a whole.

Based on my royalty formula, the Founding 21 would all have an incentive to look inhouse first to find solutions, before bringing in an additional company to the Engine.

Each founding member of the Engine will also be the 21 founding users, earning a residual revenue from those commissions and royalties.

To give perspective, the Pongo company will be one of the Engine's founding members earning 1/21 of the Engine's portion of the royalty pie and also a founding user earning commissions and royalties. This revenue stream will be enough to fund the Pongo company's entire corporate operations. That is the same potential revenue stream I am offering to each founding member of the Pongo Launch Engine.

If I were to draw out a picture of the Pongo company, as a whole, I would create a large circle. Inside the Pongo company, there is another massive circle for the Pongo Engine which almost fills the entire company circle, symbolizing that the bulk of the Pongo company is actually the Engine, which is composed of technology under licensed royalty which actually runs everything in Pongo.

The Pongo Engine circle would look like a gigantic pie, with 21 slices at the beginning. Once the Founding 21 are meeting confidentially, under contract to explore building Pongo, I will share how my patent pending business systems and processes work and expand accordingly.

Pongo's company role is to administer the exponential pre-planned growth of the Engine. The Engine and its capabilities will grow fast. It will take on a life of its own, for lack of a better phrase.

The Engine's growth and formula isn't dependent on me, once it's launched. It's automatic, dictated by my formula.

Pongo won't ever acquire a company to add its capabilities. This would be the antithesis of the Pongo business formula. Although, Pongo's revenue stream may someday be an incentive for members of the Engine to acquire a company, solely for the additional capabilities which they could bring to the Pongo Engine.

This unique corporate structure for Pongo, allows my Pongo Pay-Out System to funnel far more cash to the companies in the Engine and the users of Pongo. The bulk of the cash doesn't need to stay in the company, it needs to flow out to the user network, which will in turn bring about exponential growth.

The Pongo Engine at launch is a pretty simple core and a user would experience what would seem to be a simple in look, powerful in application Pongo overlay, with all the content flowing through the Happily Highly Monetized network, generating cash in every moment a user is participating in Pongo.

The core Engine can easily operate in every language we can translate, as fast as we can translate into a new language. The faster we can translate to every language on earth, the faster the Engine expands to reach a new market. The Pongo mission is to serve every person in every language everywhere on earth -- all of them.

Once the Pongo Engine is launched, the growth in capabilities of the Engine takes on a life of its own. Pongo company administers the additional capabilities, identifying what needs to be added to the Engine to meet the mission of connecting every device for every person -- every device.

With each additional Engine capability, the members of the Engine continue to have an incentive to look inhouse first for the additional capability prior to bringing in an additional company to the Engine.

Although the launch is simple and basic, allowing it to be replicated easily around the world, the Engine will likely see a growth unlike any other tech company created, because of my unique Pongo formula.

Pongo may redefine the concept of "scale." Scaling for Pongo will come from multiple elements: new markets reached through translation; new users coming on board in the existing markets; and the growing capabilities of the Pongo Engine.

The goal of the mission statement is to create a network where nobody wants or needs to leave the Pongo Engine. The longer we keep a user in the Engine the more cash is flowing to the network, as every moment is Happily Highly Monetized.

From our mission, Pongo must ultimately be both a personal and a business solution, to fulfill creating a communication network connecting every device for every person -- both work and play.

The ultimate task and goal of fulfilling the mission statement is so massive in its final scope, it would be ludicrous to build the full network out for launch. Thus, Pongo's launch focuses on a simple basic task of doing two things perfectly, completely, from start to finish, big to small.

In fact, these two tasks are so simple in form and functionality, the Pongo Engine for launch could probably be built in four to six months, once I have an agreement with 21 families of companies to come together to build it.

5

Pongo's Launch Engine

6 THE OPPORTUNITIES PONGO WOULD CREATE WOULD BE LIFE 99
CHANGING FOR PEOPLE -- AND WE'D PICK UP A BUNCH OF UN-
TAPPED CASH CURRENTLY SITTING UNSPENT ON THE TABLE.

Remember, this is all digital and every digital system Pongo needs to launch has already been created.

To describe Pongo at launch, I'd draw out for you a big cross or plus sign -- a vertical and horizontal line intersecting somewhere in the middle.

The vertical line up and down is the cash flow, from start to finish. The horizontal line is the content, from biggest to smallest.

Vertical Cash Flow

Let's take a box of Procter & Gamble Tide or a Ford F-250 as our example for the vertical, up and down, start to finish line.

Pongo PayOut - my Happily Highly Monetized system -- generates cash from the box of Tide leaving Procter & Gamble manufacturing facility all the way through the network of interactions to the ultimate paying customer who goes to Kroger to buy the box of Tide or has Kroger deliver the box of Tide. Pongo PayOut handles everything digital through that process. All those dealing with and touching that box

| 29 |

of Tide would use the Pongo Engine to manage and handle all transactions.

The same goes for the F-250 leaving Ford, going through the network to the ultimate dealer where the customer receives and pays for their new Ford F-250.

Thus, Pongo Engine is built to handle all digital transactions from co-op advertising, marketing, transportation, distribution, warehousing, stocking, shelf placement, sales, cash exchange upon sale and delivery. The Pongo Engine would take a corresponding small piece of the action to handle all digital transactions going through the system -- strategically priced less than the current systems used.

Not all aspects must be included in the first initial launch of the Pongo Engine. We will build out for launch what can be efficiently, effectively and completely sewn together for a full operating system, while analyzing certain aspects which could be launched in a later phase. The Engine must be complete at launch in its core functions. The dream Engine comes later.

The goal would be to make it cheaper and more efficient to utilize Pongo to handle the entire process than it would be to utilize numerous other various systems. If the goal is achieved, it is logical for all those involved with the process to choose Pongo as the preferred system.

Pongo will be driven to sell. Yes, Pongo makes a small amount of money from advertising and marketing. Pongo's big cash prize comes when Pongo sells the box of Tide or F-250. The local high school football team and local news source broadcasting their game, celebrates bigtime when a Ford F-250 sells during their football game. Procter & Gamble may find it sells more boxes of Tide during high school football every Friday night than it does at any other moment during the week.

Horizontal Content Flow

The horizontal line, biggest to smallest, is the content flowing through the Pongo Engine. This is the NFL football game, Fox News broadcast, Paramount movie, all the way down to a small-town high school football game, local news live broadcast of a car crash at the corner, individual conversation with a friend and personal photo saved in a user's private vault.

Every bit of content is making money from every part of the sales transaction. It all turns into commissions and royalties flowing out to the network involved accordingly.

Literally, everyone makes money by using Pongo to do everything they are already doing for free or paying to do. Pongo is flipping the script.

Because the content is all connected under contract, any news story, even on a small local level, can spike quickly into the biggest news story of the world instantly. And nobody has to run around seeking permission to run a video or story. The compensation stays with the creator, no matter how far reaching the content travels.

When I am asking Procter & Gamble to come onboard to build out the Pongo Launch Engine, I'm wanting P&G to help build a system that they will use, but will be available for use by every big manufacturer similar to P&G all the way down to Vicky who knits awesome woolen hats and mittens to market and sell.

By the way, Vicky sells her hand-knitted woolen hats for $60 around here. She could fetch $700 from someone in New York City. Pongo would find her buyers.

I'm asking Ford to join me in building this system, for Ford to use, as well as every manufacturer with a dealer network.

I'm seeking Kroger to be part of the original 21 families of companies, to build a full complete system they will use, yet brings the power and functionality of this communications network to a small neighborhood store, which couldn't afford to procure and build this system themselves for their little store.

Pongo brings the power and potential of the biggest and puts it into the hands of the smallest. Pongo actually will change lives and enrich local communities. It will change real lives with real opportunity.

As a small-town newspaper publisher I must be able to reach up and grab Tide co-op advertising dollars from Procter & Gamble through my local grocery store newspaper inserts, in order for my print edition to survive. Pongo does that. It's all digital now. It's 2021. We need to build this digital system.

Conversely, although I only intimately see the viewer experience and don't have purview to NFL, Fox and CBS financial books, the biggest content providers need to have the financial ability to reach down to the smallest local advertiser. That need is going to grow and for some large corporations such need will become desperate in the future.

Let me give you a real life example I see daily in my living room. One of the services I use is Smoogle-Boogle's TubeyTV to watch NFL football games, along with Fox's Tucker Carlson and CBS's Norah O'Donnell. I give Smoogle-Boogle a sick, twisted, outrageous amount of my cash every month to watch a few of the channels on their one dimensional streaming service TubeyTV.

I know personally the amount of cash my small community spent on local advertising. I was the recipient of their cash. I also know, from the local ads I'm fed from Smoogle-Boogle, Bluebookey-Facey Thing, Fox and CBS how much of the advertising dollars I received at my local newspaper are being spent by my local advertisers on these large advertising services. The answer is virtually none.

When I stopped publishing my local newspaper, my advertisers stopped spending money on advertising. It's not that they wanted to stop, they just no longer had an easy local option. All of those dollars are sitting on the table -- still -- waiting for someone to pick them up.

The big online advertising companies are receiving a tiny portion of my previous advertising dollars. I'm not talking about pennies on the dollar -- it's far less. A mere small fraction of a penny on the local advertising dollar is currently being given by local businesses in my community to the dominant internet advertising solutions. The rest is still sitting on the table.

Smoogle-Boogle and Bluebookey-Facey Thing aren't taking much cash from my community in advertising.

This isn't unique to my community. This same thing is happening in every community which lost its local news source in the last few decades.

Small businesses want to advertise. They beg to advertise. I know. I sold them their ads.

The flip side of this discussion is that the executives at NFL, CBS and Fox probably have no idea how many black screens of non-advertising are being lost during their broadcasts on streaming services. I'll tell you. I watch it. I'm not afraid to tell you the truth.

Let's use, for example, a playoff football game at the end of the NFL season I just watched. Roger Goodell and Rupert Murdoch would likely be sick to watch the blank screen on my TV during the Fox broadcast of the NFL playoff game. The screen isn't fully blank, it says something about a commercial advertisement is supposed to go here. It has a swirly thing going around the Fox logo. It has a stupid repeating ditty playing "ding dong ding dong ding dong" as the swirly swirls the Fox logo for 30 seconds.

As I watch this on my TV, I think about the local burger restaurant down the street that would love to have their ad seen by everyone in my community watching the playoff game. If there was the ability to push a button during the local burger ad while watching the game, we'd all push it and instantly order a burger right now. NFL, Fox and everyone else involved would make money from the sale of the local burger at the local burger joint. NFL and Fox can't reach my former advertisers, using their current systems. There's no system out there which does it. Don't lie to me and tell me that TubeyTV does this. I know personally that they don't. TubeyTV swirls the swirly going "ding dong" around the Fox logo on the NFL playoff game telling me that they don't have the system and sales reps to fill ad space for an NFL playoff game. The ads they do jump in with are definitely not tailored for me and my community.

The crazy aspect, because of the logo on the screen, most in the public would think it's Fox's fault there's a blank screen. They don't realize it's actually high tech TubeyTV which doesn't have a tech solution. I know whose fault it is, because the next commercial is a house ad for TubeyTV.

Right now, when I'm watching Norah O'Donnell and I'm sold on Tide's "The Amazing Clean You Love" concept, I want to push a button right now and have my box of Tide in my next grocery shipment from Kroger -- paid for, ready to go, with a royalty and commission going out to Sinclair Broadcasting, KTVL Channel 10 in Medford, CBS and Norah.

I can't.

A system hasn't been launched with a formula to allow Sinclair and CBS to earn a commission and royalty from the sale of the box of Tide at Kroger, when it's purchased during their news broadcast as a result of the great sales job of "The Amazing Clean You Love" advertisement.

I want sales now. I want an instant response. I want to sell a product or service immediately upon a advertising sales job working. I want the box of Tide in the sales cart now.

Our world now expects instant tech response. We don't want to leave what we are doing in one platform and jump to a different device to start a new process, which likely is interrupted by something else which pops up. Click it, do it, move on, is the mantra of the day.

A little while ago, finally, the media made a big deal about the launch of the little box in the corner of my TV screen. I was worried that someone was figuring out how to make the Pongo Engine happen. I made sure I was watching my TV when it was launching that evening.

Sure enough, there was a funky little box in the corner of my TV with an "i" to push for more information during a Ford commercial. I pushed my "i" to see what happened. I wanted to know if I could buy the truck being advertised. Up came another funky box on my "smart" TV that gave the Ford general website. I tried pushing something to make my "smart" TV go there. No response. I jumped on a different device, my "smart" phone, and went to a web browser to type in "ford.com" that I had been given on my "smart" TV. Of course, Ford didn't know I was showing up to their website because of their funky "i" box. They didn't let me actually buy the truck. Ford had no idea that I wanted to buy a truck.

The "i" experiment fell apart and became silly, because I couldn't instantly buy the actual truck when I was sold on the concept of owning "Built Ford Tough." It's 2021, folks. I should be able to instantly buy the product I'm sold on when using my "smart" devices. We don't have a complete system, however, to allow this, yet.

The entire process is digital, from Ford all the way to my "smart" TV, however, none of the pieces in that digital process have been connected together into one Engine. I will finally have a smart TV and a smart-phone when Pongo launches.

All the technology is digital and already created. We just need to have a corporate quilting bee and enjoy some pie.

The ViacomCBS, Fox Corporation/News Corp, Activision Blizzard, Verizon and Los Angeles Times families have built out nearly all of the broadcast side.

NewTek knows intimately how that process is brought down to a small user application, including setting up greenscreen on the high school football field sideline for a professional high school football half-time report. I know, I've used NewTek's TriCaster to try and launch this concept on a small scale to make it big. It can't start small. It must start big.

The entire process is digital. It's all been created already. No one has yet to sew together all of the digital pieces and parts to make it happen. And the cash currently being left on the table would more than make it worth the while to build Pongo so it can finally happen. #GoPongo

The opportunities Pongo would create would be life changing for people -- and we'd pick up a bunch of unspent cash currently waiting on the table.

Pongo's PayOut System is My Golden Special Sauce

" CURRENTLY, WE ARE SELLING OUR PRIVATE PARTS FOR PEN-
NIES AS THE DIGITAL BUSINESS MODEL. RATHER THAN THE
USER'S PRIVATE INFORMATION BEING THE PRODUCT SOLD,
PONGO GOES BACK TO ACTUAL GOODS AND SERVICES CON-
SUMED BY THE USERS. WE SELL REAL STUFF, REAL SERVICES.
PONGO TAKES THE INTERNET BACK TO A TRADITIONAL FORM
OF MARKETING GOODS AND SERVICES, WHILE HARNESSING
THE POWER OF THE INTERNET TO SUPER-CHARGE THE SALES
OF GOODS AND SERVICES. "

. . .

[A Patent Pending for the business systems and processes of the Pongo Engine is owned and filed by Daniel Webster. This chapter has been withheld from this public ebook, and can only be accessed exclusively through a signed written agreement between Daniel Webster with the prospective 21 Pongo Founding Engine members.]

. . .

7

Pongo's Algorithm Separates Pongo from the Rest of the Silliness

THE **PONGO** FORMULA KEEPS THE USER IN **PONGO** AS LONG AS POSSIBLE, TO KEEP THE CONSTANT HAPPILY, HIGHLY MONE-TIZED SYSTEM CRANKING OUT CASH FOR THE NETWORK. IT ALSO SEEKS TO KEEP A USER INSIDE A BRAND, TO FURTHER A BRAND MAKING MORE MONEY. MOST IMPORTANTLY, IT EN-SURES THAT EVERY USER RECEIVES A PLEASANT, NON-OFFEN-SIVE EXPERIENCE WITH PONGO, WHICH KEEPS A USER PREFERRING TO STAY IN PONGO, RATHER THAN JUMPING OUT TO ANOTHER, LESS CAPABLE PLATFORM.

. . .

[A Patent Pending for the business systems and processes of the Pongo Engine is owned and filed by Daniel Webster. This chapter has been withheld from this public ebook, and can only be accessed exclusively through a signed written agreement between Daniel Webster with the prospective 21 Pongo Founding Engine members.]

. . .

I Learned the Hard Way -- Keep Some Things a Secret Until the Right Time

" CERTAIN ELEMENTS, I'VE NEVER SPOKEN OF OR RELEASED TO "
ANYONE, EVER. IT'S MY SAFETY NET TO RETAIN MY OWNERSHIP
AND CONTROL UNTIL I HAVE 21 COMPANIES ALL AGREEING IN
CONTRACT TO PURSUE MY PONGO PLAN. I LEARNED THE HARD
WAY.

The school of hardknocks hurts sometimes. It also is a great way to learn. My grandpa taught me that real-world education is more expensive than college.

In order to launch Pongo, I need to tell the world about the plan, yet, never speak to anyone about certain proprietary secrets I must protect, until the right point in time. It's my way of protecting my idea, my vision, my business plan, my patent pending and copyrighted intellectual property. You are reading this approach in this #GoPongo book.

Certain elements, I've never spoken of or released to anyone, ever. It's my safety net to secure my ownership and control until I have 21 companies all agreeing in contract to pursue my Pongo plan. I own the patent pending for the business systems and processes of the Pongo Engine. I learned the hard way.

After law school, I decided to launch my plan for Our Times, a national, regionalized gay and lesbian newspaper. It filled a desperate need. If it had launched, it would currently be the largest print -- and now digital -- newspaper in the world.

I wasn't born with a gift to think small. It's not within my nature.

I put everything into a business plan believing my idea was powerful enough to cause someone to move forward with me and back my Our Times project.

With everything I do, I analyze the minutiae of the details and see how each element plays out with each other piece of the formula.

Such was the case with Our Times. It was created specifically to be a gay and lesbian regionalized newspaper. The elements of Our Times uniquely addressed aspects of the gay and lesbian community.

At that juncture, in 1996, the term "gay and lesbian" was all inclusive. Everyone was included in the concept of "gay and lesbian" if they were supportive and part of the "community." It would be similar to the scenes along the routes of a "pride parade" featuring everyone that supported the "community." LGBTQIA hadn't been contemplated yet as a necessary and valid acronym replacing the term "gay and lesbian," however, it means the same thing today.

I exclusively submitted my Our Times business plan to Mr. Rupert Murdoch at News Corp, after which, Los Angeles Times.

Mr. Murdoch personally rejected my proposal at the time. Some personal rejection letters are tremendously valuable to me.

The Los Angeles Times signed a Non Disclosure Agreement (NDA) submitted to them by my attorney.

The Los Angeles Times was in a desperate financial position in that era, prior to its ultimate bankruptcy.

On March 25, 1997, Los Angeles Times Senior Vice President Marketing and New Business Development Robert N. Brisco, sent me, via my attorney, a letter rejecting my Our Times proposal to the Los Angeles Times and Times Mirror.

I moved back to my small town to buy my hometown newspaper instead.

One morning, having put all of my eggs in my one local newspaper basket, I was thumbing through my edition of Editor & Publisher magazine. There it was. An article about Los Angeles Times launching its new regionalized newspaper, Our Times. OMG.

Former Los Angeles Times Publisher Mark Hinckley Willes announced to his staff that he had an "epiphany" and the idea of Our Times came to him.

I call "bull" on the epiphany notion. My Our Times business plan was his "epiphany." My mind gave Mr. Willes his epiphany, not his.

The Los Angeles Times concept, their obvious business plan, took nearly all the elements of my business plan for Our Times, gutted the gay and lesbian part, and launched it without me, as merely a regionalized newspaper of general circulation in the Southern California market.

Well, buggers.

Desperate people at desperate corporations will do desperate things.

I had a choice. A legal fight with the Los Angeles Times would be viscous, go for years and be all consuming. On the other hand, I had just put everything I had into the struggling local newspaper I was purchasing and dedicating my life to turn around and make it successful.

If I fought with the LA Times, I would be distracted from my most important, all consuming work at my Pioneer Press.

It was one or the other. The Los Angeles Times could afford a bigger, better legal team than I could at the time.

I had to let it go and walk away from the alleged theft of intellectual property, if I wanted my little local newspaper to make it. My community needed me to fight for them, not fight against the LA Times.

The gay and lesbian community would never know what they lost -- until this book came out.

I moved on.

I knew at the time, the Los Angeles Times was doomed with their Our Times swipe. They couldn't ultimately make it successful. It would be a goose egg on Willis' face. Much of my plan was specifically tailored to be successful based on the uniqueness of the gay and lesbian market. Major elements of my business plan couldn't work outside of that specific market. My Our Times plan couldn't be transferred and used by a general audience.

I knew that the Los Angeles Times would be spending a bunch of cash on a foolish, silly, greedy alleged theft of my property ownership. They reportedly spent $5 to $7 million on their Our Times project, yielding $2 million in revenue. A far cry from the prospective spreadsheets I submitted with my Our Times business plan.

I somewhat enjoyed watching the Los Angeles Times' little Our Times experiment crash and burn a few years later. I could have told them it would. I laughed.

I also knew that elements of what my mind conceives cannot be shared until the right moment, if I want to protect my unique, intricate vision.

Thus, certain elements of this Pongo plan, although it appears I am publishing it for the world, actually can't be launched without me.

Those who hook up with me get my mind and can launch Pongo.

The other reason I am taking this odd, ultra-public approach to launching Pongo, is if anyone, anywhere, in any context tries to steal elements of my Pongo plan, I want the world to scream "Hey, that's Daniel Webster's Pongo Plan. How dare you use that without him. You thief."

I didn't have that when I submitted Our Times. This time I will. I won't make that foolish mistake again.

You, the world, will be my ultimate protector this time to ensure nobody steals Pongo. Smiling. TYIA.

It's also one of the reasons I want the Los Angeles Times to be part of my Founding 21 Pongo Launch Engine. I want to do it right this time.

For my lifetime, the LA Times has been my favorite daily newspaper in the world. They still are. They will continue to be.

My Big News Experiment on Mark's Bluebookey-Facey Thing

"I AM THE LARGEST MEDIA, BY FAR, IN MY COUNTY, OVER-
WHELMINGLY BEATING THE HUGE MEDIA CONGLOMERATE
NEWSPAPER HOLDINGS STILL LEFT AND STRUGGLING TO SUR-
VIVE HERE IN MY COUNTY. BUT, I CAN'T MAKE MONEY. MARK
WON'T LET ME."

After I shut down the printing press for my weekly newspaper Pioneer Press, I watched intimately the ramifications of its demise on my
community. It ripped our community apart. The impact was heart-
breaking.

Unlike big city journalists, I would see my readers personally at the
grocery store and gas station. Some wanted to beat the you-know-what
out of me because I closed their newspaper. Some cried. All begged me
to do something to bring back their newspaper.

When they lost their newspaper, some didn't know that their friend
died because they didn't see the obituary, and they blamed me for it.
It's not pleasant being punched by an old lady in the grocery store, who
fully means it, because she missed her friend's funeral. I had to take it.

I decided to launch local news pages on Bluebookey-Facey Thing, to
somewhat give my community a continued connection. I call my journalism "news-lite" on that platform.

When an emergency transpired locally, I was the go-to news source for instant information the community couldn't get elsewhere. It was their most desperate need. In all seriousness, devastating wildfires built my large local following.

A community experiences less angst, the freak-out level comes down dramatically, when they are given immediate, local information regarding the real threats affecting their lives.

Going live from a forest fire or flood approaching one of my towns, brings calm, strategic reactions, when they know exactly where the threat is located and the severity of their personal peril.

The loss of local news has an impactful harm on a community. The harm is real.

I live in Siskiyou County, with a population of 45,000. My four local pages Yreka News, Scott Valley News, Mount Shasta News and Siskiyou News have a total of 36,831 followers. That's 81 percent of the population.

I am the largest media, by far, in my county, overwhelmingly beating the PannettFannett newspaper holdings still left and struggling to survive here in my county. PannettFannett controls nearly all print in my region.

But, I can't make money.

My former weekly newspaper readership comprised approximately 80 percent of my market's population -- a valley with 6,000 people. Big city publishers are gobsmacked by my 80 percent.

Although my local news following is a tremendously high percentage of my population, I can't make a cent from my news published exclusively using the Bluebookey-Facey Thing platform.

I've tried using Twitter and Bluebookey-Facey Thing's acquired GramItInAnInstant. Twitter is worthless for small town news delivery -- it works to get quick news-esque tidbits out on a national and worldwide scale. Many in my community may be on Twitter, however, they don't care if I've ever posted tiny ditties on my Scott Valley News and Yreka News accounts on Twitter.

On occasion, I will also post my shorter stories and photos on GramItInAnInstant. The response is tremendously underwhelming. Yawn.

I gave away one of my pages, Klamath Falls News, to a former employee, Brian Gailey, to do an experiment to see if he could make a living in that market using Bluebookey-Facey Thing. It has been a tough go. Although Brian has built up a large following in the Klamath Basin, in Southern Oregon, he must use multiple platforms and a website to sell advertising packages encompassing his entire network of platforms to support his family. It is not ideal, it's labor intensive, it doesn't provide him with commensurate cash for the size of his audience.

One day, I saw my county supervisor at the gas station.

"Daniel, what you are doing with your news is a labor of love for the community, isn't it?" he asked.

"Yes, it is."

"So you don't get paid for doing your work?"

No, [Bluebookey-Facey Thing] sucks. I can't make any money on it. It's a stupid non-solution for news. It's the only solution right now for local news, just to keep us together on a local level," I told my county supervisor.

Yes, I'm the largest media in my entire county and I'm not making a cent doing it. I can't. Mark won't let me. I must do it as a labor of love. Most journalists and news outfits don't publish news as a labor of love, as it's a stupid business plan.

Journalists can't make a living covering local news digitally, because Pongo hasn't launched. #GoPongo

Pongo is a Talking Dog

" OUR LIVE LOGO PONGO IS EMBLEMATIC OF THE ADVANCING "
TECHNOLOGY OF THE PONGO ENGINE. PONGO DEFINES AND IS
THE EXAMPLE OF THE CUTTING EDGE CAPABILITIES OF THE
PONGO ENGINE.

When the Pongo vision hit me in the late 1990s on what I had to build to replace my local newspaper, I knew the system had to be live video centric and voice driven inorder to comport with the direction I viewed the internet going eventually.

Pongo would have to talk.

Folks had to be able to talk to Pongo.

That's where I came up with the name Pongo.

Pongo was my dog.

Pongo is big, black and white, probably a cross between a Great Dane and Dalmatian. Pongo is friendly, fun, happy, loves to play and sleep. Pongo cares. If computer-generated imagery (CGI) allows Pongo to jump on the couch, Pongo will hang out on the couch.

No worries. Pongo is a digital talking dog and it won't hurt the couch when it sits next to you and is the most hypoallergenic dog a person can enjoy.

Pongo is our live logo. When you ask Pongo to find anything, it instantly responds with whatever you want. You and Pongo can talk about stuff.

Pongo is what you push, click or talk with to do anything in the system. All the capabilities of Pongo come from Pongo. The simplicity of the talking dog will define the easy, clean nature of the Pongo network.

Pongo is an "it" and has no gender nor a need to relieve itself. No complications.

Pongo speaks in every language we serve. Ultimately, Pongo will speak every language on earth.

Pongo is emblematic of the advancing technology of the Pongo Engine. Pongo defines and is the example of the cutting edge CGI capabilities of the Pongo Engine. If Pongo, our live logo, can do it, you will find that the Pongo Engine is capable of doing it as well.

Likely, Activision Blizzard, one of my prospective 21 Pongo Launch Engine companies, will be one of our tech cores pushing the visual-virtual Pongo experience, thus pushing the capabilities of our live Pongo logo, the talking dog.

If CGI is capable of taking a digital dog on a walk, you can take Pongo for a walk and chat as you stroll through the neighborhood. Your Pongo live logo dog will learn a users personality, needs, desires, topics, and shopping preferences. Artificial intelligence is fabulous.

You won't need a leash or one of those handy-dandy plastic bags to carry around.

If a dog freaks you out, no worries, the talking dog can hide in the background and not be visible. No freaking out on Pongo.

If you aren't interacting with Pongo at the time, it sleeps in the corner.

11

Pongo is Happily, Highly Monetized

" PONGO'S GOAL IS TO MAKE PEOPLE HAPPY MAKING MONEY "
FROM DOING WHAT THEY ALREADY ARE WILLING TO DO BE-
GRUDGINGLY, WITH ANNOYANCE, WHILE SWEARING, USING A
DIFFERENT PLATFORM.

Users hate highly monetized online systems, especially if they must already pay a monthly fee. It's a real hate.

For Pongo to have a highly monetized system, it must produce happiness in the users when they are participating in their usage being highly monetized.

When encountering ads on a streaming service one is already paying good money to access, users want to push "Skip Ad" as they mumble "they've already taken enough bloody money from me."

First of all, that system is monetized, making money off you. It's not highly monetized, in comparison to Pongo monetizing every moment possible. It's definitely not Happily, Highly Monetized, based on your mumbling swear words as you use their system.

If I sit down in the evening to enjoy streaming TV and do my smartphone social media stuff as I'm watching, all in perfect sync on Pongo, I turn from annoyed to happy when my normal routine pays for my latte. I become especially happy if my latte joint uses Pongo and has my latte automatically ready and paid for, based on my safe, secure automatic order placed when my Pongo car gets close enough to my Pongo equipped favorite coffee drive through.

It's all digital. It's all been created. It's 2021, folks. Let's connect it all together.

A smart Pongo user becomes happier when they share the daily coffee special at their favorite shop with all their folks nearby, so when their friends buy their coffee, the smart Pongo user makes cash from the sale, because they were part of the network to make the coffee sale happen.

Pongo's goal is to make people happy making money from doing what they already are willing to do begrudgingly, with annoyance, while swearing. Think about the amount of screaming profanities at inanimate digital devices we will eliminate when we launch Pongo. That alone will make the world a better, happier place.

12

Pongo's Moral Responsibility to Save Local News Worldwide

" WE HAVE BECOME POLARIZED BECAUSE WE'VE DESTROYED "
THAT WHICH BRINGS US TOGETHER IN UNITY. LOCAL NEWS ON
A COMMUNITY LEVEL IS WHERE WE FIND OUR UNITY. IT BRINGS
US TOGETHER.

When my vision for Pongo came to me, I knew it came with multiple moral responsibilities.

One of the greatest of these moral responsibilities was to save local news worldwide. This became my personal calling, challenge, and culmination of my life's work.

From the time I understood what I needed to build to now, when all the pieces and parts have now been created, I have watched thousands upon thousands of local news services go out of business in the United States, leaving their communities without a heartbeat. The number of local news services which have died worldwide would be staggering.

There's a price to pay for the loss of local news. We are experiencing it in our reality. We probably don't know that the death of local news is to blame.

I hear a bunch of talk about "polarization." I hear talking heads screaming "we are so polarized." Our society has indeed become polarized. The impact is real and we know it.

Why?

To be harsh with my assessment, the polarization we are seeing nationwide and worldwide is not a political issue. It's just the symptom we are watching of the real problem playing out.

We have become polarized because we destroyed that which brought us together in unity.

Hyperlocal and microlocal news on a community level is where we find our unity. It brings us together.

We all root for our home team. We all come together for a local kid we all know struggling with cancer. We all celebrate our local superstar for their local achievement. We all weep when someone in our community sobs. We all rejoice in a local joy. We all rise up and come together in one unified purpose to achieve a local common goal.

On a hyperlocal, microlocal and nanolocal level we experience unity.

We are not polarized locally.

Hyperlocal, microlocal and nanolocal news brought us all together, in unity.

We killed local news. We killed unity.

Of course, we became polarized.

We no longer have local news to show us how unified we truly are, such that we think we are no longer unified, as we now only view large polarizing issues, which we actually can't individually do anything about in a meaningful manner.

We created this mess when we didn't replace our hyperlocal and microlocal news sources with a viable digital solution to deliver news on the internet. It's our fault. I wish every journalist who speaks or writes about polarization, follows up with the explanation that we became polarized when local news died.

I have a moral responsibility to change that. Pongo, by virtue of being launched by me, a small town news publisher, is born with that moral responsibility.

Therefore, if I would adjust the Pongo Launch Engine vertical and horizontal lines to intersect at the focal point of our primary purpose, I would adjust the lines to cross at the point of successfully delivering hyperlocal, microlocal and nanolocal news to a small town and intimate community.

What is a Small Town?

Prior to 2020, the most difficult task in communicating this Pongo concept was that we all live in a small town.

What small town do you live in?

No, the answers "LA" and "NYC" are not valid. Los Angeles and New York aren't small towns, they contain numerous small towns.

You know the real answer after 2020, because your world became focused on your small town.

Let me ask again. What small town do you live in?

"Miracle Mile," would be a valid answer for a location in Los Angeles.

"Oh, sweet, Los Angeles High School is in your small town. Go Romans! There's a Kroger owned store, Ralphs, in your small town," I would reply.

Our lives became more hyperlocal and microlocal centric last year, out of necessity.

"What is your microlocal newspaper in Miracle Mile?" I would follow up.

"The Los Angeles Times."

It would likely be financially ludicrous for Dr. Patrick Soon-Shiong to build out a digital system to serve every hyperlocal and microlocal small town in the LA Times news market. On a larger level, they tried it previously with Our Times. It would be silly to hire the sales staff and journalists to cover sports and local news around the Los Angeles High School small town neighborhood. Dr. Soon-Shiong has oodles of small towns under his wings at the Los Angeles Times -- hundreds of them. I've intimately analyzed it for him already.

Yet, the LA Times brand is leaving a tremendous amount of cash sitting on the hyperlocal and microlocal tables throughout his markets, because his business model doesn't reach down that deep.

I have specifically identified more than 15,000 specific hyperlocal and microlocal markets in the United States, which accounts for all communities and neighborhoods down to 7,000 in size, to launch on Pongo. There are also approximately 16,000 high schools in the U.S., most identified by MaxPreps Sports.

Pongo allows even one of the nation's largest and most prestigious newspapers to do the deep dive into microlocal small towns throughout big city markets. It's easy. It's cheap.

My Pongo formula should produce a $80,000 to $100,000 revenue for a hyperlocal or microlocal journalist focusing on a small town, similar in size to my small town in the shadow of Northern California's Mt. Shasta. The same formula works in the small town of Miracle Mile in LA, West Chelsea in New York City, or Allandale Park in Austin, Texas. Some skyscrapers could qualify as a small town.

I live in a hardcore Sinclair market. The company dominates the Designated Market Areas (DMA) in my neck of the woods. I actually live in the middle of two DMAs. My local Sinclair stations are KTVL in the Medford/Klamath Falls Ore. DMA and KRCR in the Chico/Redding Calif. DMA. These DMAs are ranked #139 and #132, respectively. They aren't the biggies.

Sinclair is currently earning revenue from approximately one microlocal advertiser in my former newspaper market. Just one. That one advertiser lost both its local weekly and daily newspapers. That one advertiser used to give me their advertising dollars. They started advertising with Sinclair after their local newspapers bit the dust.

The rest of the local advertising dollars are sitting on the table. Sinclair can't get the cash. They don't have a business plan and formula to get it. The cash is waiting for Pongo to launch. Sinclair will be able to do a deep dive into my microlocal market through advertising and news coverage with Pongo, as Sinclair will throughout the country. It's cheap. It's automatic.

I will jump into Pongo's strength for branding in an upcoming chapter. Both Sinclair and Los Angeles Times could use it effectively. Everyone else will use Pongo's branding capabilities, as well.

Let's be frank, on many levels we are currently looking at a wounded society, because we've lost so much of what brought us together in unity. We heal when communities unify. This balm of unity comes when we bring back hyperlocal and microlocal news, giving communities a successful local news solution.

Pongo's on a mission to heal broken communities, across this country, around the world. There's hope. It's coming.

13

Biggest to Smallest -- Worldwide to Private

" I DESIGNED PONGO TO PAY FOR A NEWS SERVICE TO CARE FOR "
A HYPERLOCAL OR MICROLOCAL COMMUNITY SIMILARLY SITU-
ATED TO MINE -- 6,000 TO 7,000 FOLKS. A FULL TIME INCOME
SHOULD BE ABLE TO BE GENERATED BY COVERING A POPULA-
TION GROUP THIS SIZE.

Pongo is designed for someone in a hyperlocal market, and some microlocal markets, to cover their hyperlocal area and earn a prospective $80,000 to $100,000 income from working their market full time with their content. Pongo must be a real business opportunity for a real person doing their real work in their real world. That's one of the primary ways Pongo will change and empower real lives.

There are journalists in my community who would likely love that opportunity for income. Some of them used to work for me and the corporate owned former daily. The same is true around the country.

A currently operating local newspaper would have a turnkey solution to literally turn off their printing press and with the push of the Pongo button and at $2 a month be able to turn on their new business serving their current customers, successfully.

My Happily Highly Monetized system gives greater or lesser business opportunity according to the scope of the content target reach.

A worldwide content provider, producing good stuff the world cares about, could make a massive bank drop from Pongo. An individual solely using Pongo for personal use would likely pay for their Pongo subscription and buy their lattes with the revenue earned from Pongo.

The brilliant financial minds at Tesla and Ford will be able to analyze the Pongo PayOut System to determine if they can give a car away for a $2 Pongo subscription, if the automobile is equipped and using the Pongo Engine onboard for its internet services. I think they will be able to, depending on the time spent driving the car everyday. It will be an interesting analysis. I look forward to seeing the results.

Pongo goes from worldwide all the way down to intimate and personal content creation. There are many steps along the way, primarily in the local realm. Because Pongo dives so deep, I needed to add some terms to the mix. Pongo will redefine many aspects of "local."

Worldwide

We all understand the concept of worldwide and nationwide, as it applies to content target markets. Conceivable, NFL, Wall Street Journal and Los Angeles Times are all worldwide content providers, most of the time.

Language Group

The next level down from worldwide is language group. There are more Mandarin speakers than live in China, of course. There are more general English communicators than live in specific English speaking countries. The United States has many language groups within its borders.

The Pongo core at launch is English and translated into every language on earth, with those languages translated into every other language.

Wycliffe Bible Translators has translated enough of the Bible into 3,415 languages around the world to use artificial intelligence applications of its Bible translations, to bring the Pongo Engine core public interaction shell into these languages. Wycliffe is the most advanced in general translation work around the world. They've been doing it a long time. By Wycliffe being one of the 21 Pongo Launch Engine companies, Pongo conceivably could quickly launch into as many as 3,415 language groups.

Many of these language groups will be dependent on Elon Musk's SpaceX, possibly StarLink capabilities, to reach them, as I doubt there's a phone line or cell tower nearby. I've heard of some living deep in the bush, far from traditional internet access who have a smartphone. Depending on the monetary system in that language group, or lack thereof, Pongo may be operating in their local language group through bartering cryptocurrency or fruits and vegetables, water or chickens. In those markets, the Pongo company won't be earning a half a zucchini from a transaction. It's not possible. The fruits and vegetables stay local. These communities would be served by Pongo because we have a mission statement which dictates that we must. Cryptocurrency may be used to reach areas otherwise unable to be served with other financial systems.

According to Wycliffe, additionally, 3,945 languages still have no Scripture completed, with 2,014 languages still in need of translation work to begin. Wycliffe and AI experts can help me understand how many of the 3,945 languages still in work have enough done to launch Pongo in those languages. It's possible that upwards to 7,360 languages could be available to translate the Pongo core shell.

It's far greater than the reach of 108 and 100 languages the two tech giants are operating in now.

Pongo has a long way to go to get into every language everywhere on earth.

Regional

A Designated Market Area (DMA) is a good regional definition. It's already clearly established and in such wide use in the U.S., there's no point in reinventing that wheel.

KTTV, WCBS, KTVL and KRCR are good examples, as we've lightly explored above, of media in regional DMA markets.

New York Post has a worldwide audience with tremendous content covering issues around the world, yet it is a regional news source for New York.

Hyperlocal

Hyperlocal is the designation for an area within the Los Angeles Times local service area, such as Miracle Mile or the New York Post's market of West Chelsea in New York City.

My local small town newspaper operated in a hyperlocal market. I live in one of the largest counties in California, according to its land-mass. It is also one of the smallest population counties in the state. My primary market area covered a large valley -- absolutely gorgeous, by the way -- with a population of 6,000. Our county seat, Yreka in Siskiyou County, has a population of 7,000.

The county seat lost its daily newspaper. My valley lost its weekly newspaper.

I designed Pongo to pay for a news service to care for a hyperlocal or microlocal community similarly situated to mine -- 6,000 to 7,000 folks. A full time income should be able to be generated by covering a population group this size. Some skyscrapers and the block which surrounds it in New York City or Chicago are a hyperlocal small town.

There are a lot of unemployed journalists who probably need a turnkey opportunity right where they live, servicing a hyperlocal area which lost its newspaper or radio station.

Microlocal

A microlocal level market would be similar to covering sports at a local high school. An independent sports journalist/entrepreneur would probably want to cover a couple of schools, to make a good living covering sports.

Nanolocal

A nanolocal environment is getting down to a small group, such as a drama club at a high school, the quilters group, a church or civic club. The income potential at this level with Pongo would be akin to hosting a fabulous bake sale.

Intimate

Intimate designates a one on one conversation or a group chat scenario. It's what Ma Bell would do, with the technology of Verizon.

Private

Private level contains the photos I take and the videos I capture which stay in my vault. This level is private and personal. This is content created and Happily Highly Monetized so the individual user can within the extreme privacy of their Pongo Vault still generate cash, simply by participating in the Pongo PayOut System.

14

The Power of Local

" IT'S THE POWERFUL DYNAMICS AND SYNERGY OF BRINGING IT "
ALL TOGETHER IN ONE FORMULA IN MY PONGO ENGINE. IT'S
HOW THE LITTLE GUY REACHES ALL THE WAY UP TO EARN
CASH FROM PLUCKING THE FRUIT FROM THE BIGGEST, TALLEST
TREE AND THE BIGGEST, TALLEST TREE REACHES ALL THE WAY
DOWN TO SUCK THE NUTRIENTS FROM THE DEEPEST LOCAL
SOIL.

The full combined power of local advertising cash flow is in the billions of dollars and isn't being calculated in the mix. It's the forgotten cash. We are ignoring this big, untapped well of cash flow, with the currently existing business plans of the largest media and high tech companies.

There may be more money to be made from selling local ads than nationally targeted advertising. It's somewhat a hidden figure. I can give you my personal experience as a small town publisher.

Some have figured this out and offer regional advertising. I can see this in the advertisements I watch on national streaming services.

Nobody is capable of reaching down to get the hyperlocal, microlocal, nanolocal cash. They just can't, because Pongo hasn't been launched yet.

No formula exists to personally target and tailor an advertisement for an individual viewer, especially localized. We can target a location, however, the ad isn't individualized just for me. I base this assessment on the ads fed to me from the largest social media and search platforms. This is absolutely true in national television advertising, as I'm not seeing ads on CBS and Fox which are tailored just for me. The entire process is now digital, we just haven't put it all in one system to do it.

I know this. I've lived this.

This level of cash is also uncalculated with our current measuring sticks.

At my small town newspaper, there was never a calculation done -- data collected -- of my local advertising revenue amounts, which would ultimately lead to a national statistic of how much local advertising was happening on a hyperlocal, microlocal and nanolocal level. I believe this is truly an unknown quantity.

Thus, the largest well of untapped advertising and marketing cash is unknown. Yet, I know intimately, that its combined total represents a figure which is likely more than $5 billion.

We are so focused on the big advertising contracts -- Ford and P&G spend a bazillion on advertising -- that we forget about the accumulated dollars in advertising spent by the local restaurant, local grocery store, local nail salon, local family owned business.

This is the level of advertising which has been lost with the massive local newspaper shutdown and is now sitting on the table waiting to be picked up.

Pongo harvests this local cash, effectively.

What can't be calculated in a spreadsheet is the level of local loyalty an advertiser enjoys. Big and small advertisers all experience it on a local level. The largest advertisers may not know intimately that it's happening.

In order to understand it, you have to talk to a person like me. Someone who's lived it and knows first hand what happens with local advertising cash.

Local news is intensely personal, as it deals with issues which affect a reader personally, where the person lives and their intimate daily life.

So too is local advertising.

In a local news environment, local advertising is part of the local news feeling, and is treated as part of the local news experience.

A local reader considers a local ad as part of the local information which locally plays a role in their life.

Local readers and viewers, consider a local advertiser to be a local supporter of their community. The line between news and advertising blurs on a local level. Readers and viewers watch and participate in it all intimately. After all, an advertisement for their local pizza restaurant or Kroger grocery store is coming from a local business they know and shop. The local person wants to support their local business to keep them thriving in their local community. They're friends.

In a sense, we know this to be true. It's the power of co-op advertising from national advertisers reaching all the way down to a local newspaper.

What many don't realize, national advertisers become "locals" when they support the local news and become part of the local community. Ford and P&G become one of us on a local level, when we see a Tide and F-250 ad in our local news or supporting our local high school.

It's why I believe Procter & Gamble may sell more Tide during high school football games than they will during other events. P&G just became one of us on a local level, supporting our local team, when their ad is supporting local football. The national advertisers experience intense local loyalty, when they reach down to a local level.

Local loyalty translates to local sales dollars, to support the advertiser who supports us.

We support those who support us.

If you are one of us, we will go out of our way to choose your product, because your product is supporting what we care about.

Which is why Pongo will localize and make personal national advertising. Tide will be tagged with the price at my local Kroger grocery store where I shop to be added to my shopping cart. The F-250 ad from Ford is tagged with my local dealer in my hometown with the colors and options in stock ready to deliver right now.

It's a similar notion to advertisers supporting "a cause" which purchasers support.

It's the notion of advertising to the gay community, in their community, as the power to draw sales from the community the advertisement supports. Take that notion and supercharge it, when we apply it to a local level.

Right now, advertisers can't support a local community and experience local loyalty, because we've destroyed the local news market. There's no place, no format, no method to reach the local community and cause a national advertiser to become a local.

The large digital advertising options aren't selling to that market. I rarely see a local ad for my community on Bluebookey-Facey Thing or Smoogle-Boogle. It's not happening. The locals aren't giving them the advertising dollars they previously gave me. BFT and SB don't have local advertising sales reps running around selling ads, because there's no commission and royalty structure to make that happen. A local news outlet would sell those ads.

To tap into the local loyalty, there must be a formula which compensates locally driven advertising.

To squeeze as much cash out of my Pongo PayOut System, a hyperlocal or microlocal news outlet will do what local news businesses have done for centuries. They will sell local Pongo subscriptions to build a residual income, sell local advertisements which drive local sales and produce local content their community cares about.

The dynamics and synergy of my Pongo PayOut formula kicks in through the algorithm which brings all of that together on the national and worldwide Pongo Engine.

This is how a locally owned pizza business advertisement, sold by the local media outlet, shows up during an NFL football game, causing the viewer to instantly push the Pongo button to purchase the local pizza and have it delivered by their local pizza delivery driver in a few minutes to eat during the game -- with the NFL making cash from the local pizza sale.

On a national level, Pongo will be localizing the national ads, typically through a co-op advertising solution. Rather than viewing an advertisement for just Tide during the CBS national news broadcast, a local viewer will see the special price for Tide at their local Kroger location where they shop, so by pushing the Pongo buy-it-now button they are adding the box of Tide to their next shopping bag at their special local Pongo "coupon" price.

The local media outlet which sold the pizza ad and the national content creator make money from the sale of the local pizza. The national advertising sales media which sold the Tide ad makes money from the sale at the local store.

It's the powerful dynamics and synergy of bringing it all together in one formula in my Pongo Engine.

It's how the little content creator reaches all the way up to earn cash from plucking the fruit from the biggest, tallest tree and the biggest, tallest tree reaches all the way down to suck the nutrients from the deepest local soil.

It can only happen in a singular, synergistic manner with Pongo, using a complete digital system.

I would guess a Founding 21 member, such as Sinclair, is exploring the concept of doing this over digital airwaves, which will open up even more possibilities.

Patch and Sinclair can't get fully local, they can't afford it

Patch and Sinclair can't afford to go fully hyperlocal or microlocal -- their business plan won't allow it.

Sinclair is reaching down to a regional level, Patch is at a larger local and a few hyperlocal levels.

I have keenly watched the current local business formulas play out, with my mind on the difference between these systems and my Pongo plan.

Patch and Sinclair are excellent examples of companies which appear to be successfully implementing a localized business plan. Both are able to tap into local markets, and do it right.

They can't, however, go fully local. They can't afford it. Their business plan won't allow it.

Both these companies have a business plan which involves paying someone on their staff to go sell the ads and produce the content, to bring their local news to life. Both can't afford to go hardcore deep and local. Their business formula, from my vantage point, can only go down to a regional, local, sometimes hyperlocal level. They can't afford to pay the staff to produce an income at a hyperlocal or microlocal level. It won't pay for itself.

By using the Pongo system, Patch and Sinclair could begin earning money -- profitably -- from the smaller localized markets. The dynamics and power of Pongo are rich, for those large businesses which have a local business plan. With Pongo, neither Patch nor Sinclair need to employ the staff to reach a hyperlocal or microlocal market within their current local environment. They just need to be the first ones to figure out the powerful potential of branding on Pongo.

Branding on Pongo

From the Wall Street Journal to Los Angeles Times, from Patch to Sinclair, Pongo was created for branding. It may prove to be, especially for certain businesses, the greatest potential of Pongo.

Consider this.

Large national brands can cheaply and effectively take their brand down to a hyperlocal or microlocal market, profitably earning cash from the Pongo approach.

A national news brand doesn't need to hire staff to work its brand in the microlocal environment or niche market, they just have to find the right person to brand.

How many quality unemployed journalists are out there right now, as an example?

A lot.

How many would prefer to be producing work product?

Almost all of them.

How many are qualified to work for a large established brand?

Many of them.

How long does it take for an editor to make a decision on a person qualified to wear a brand?

Minutes. Just look at their previous work product and do a background check.

Pongo instantly brands. It's super easy and part of my Pongo PayOut System. And it doesn't cost more than the few minutes to pick out the right person to wear the brand.

Once a user/journalist is branded by a big brand, Pongo's algorithm prefers to keep a user in that brand, so the brand continues to make cash from the user. Encouraging brand loyalty is one of our ways of keeping users in Pongo so they don't leave the network. People love and trust their favorite brand.

Let's use my small town area. I currently publish Scott Valley News and Yreka News, two markets with approximately 6,000 to 7,000 folks. Wall Street Journal, CBS, Patch and Sinclair can't touch my neck of the woods with their business formula to pull all the content and cash from this small market.

Let's pretend for a moment that my reporting actually rises to the level qualifying me to wear the brand of Wall Street Journal, CBS, Patch or Sinclair -- LOL -- and one of these companies chooses to brand me as their own. My local news business would turn into an entirely different business opportunity if I am producing the Wall Street Journal Business Report for Scott Valley and Yreka. News Corp would be reaching deep, all the way down to my small community, pulling cash from my microlocal market. In the same manner, Sinclair can slap the Sinclair/CBS brand on me, as a qualified journalist entrepreneur in my market, through their KTVL Channel 10 CBS affiliate serving my DMA. CBS, Sinclair, KTVL don't have to put me on staff or pay me a bloody cent. They just need to use Pongo to collect their portion of cash from my royalties and commissions. Super easy, super cheap, super effective, super profitable. Oh, and Pongo handles all the "paperwork" and bank deposits for everyone.

On a local level, I would be agreeing to the code of conduct and news style of the brand. The bigger and more prestigious the brand, the greater my personal opportunity to earn. I could be branded by various brands, depending on the variety of reporting or work product.

I would have a better influence on my local community to bring my locals into a major brand than probably the brand itself. Once I bring a local into the brand as a user, the local user will likely stay longer in the brand. When I sell a local subscription for my local news service, the brand which branded me is also earning a residual revenue from my branded sale. The same goes with advertising I sell to my local advertisers. The same goes with the products my locals buy at the store. Not only do I make money from it all, the cash flows all the way up the big, tall tree to the national or worldwide brand.

Those who figure out this part of the formula first will likely be the ones to make the most cash from the Pongo Branding System.

Everything to make this network happen is already created. We have all the pieces and parts ready to put it all together in one dynamic, synergistic, powerful system. We just now have to build Pongo. It's 2021, folks. It's all digital. It's time to sew together the Pongo quilt and eat some pie.

15

The Pongo Bank Vault

" THE WORLD NEEDS PONGO, BECAUSE THE WORLD NEEDS TO "
EXIST IN A SAFE, SECURE ENVIRONMENT.

Pongo is a bank. We literally need to quickly create a bank.

Once the Founding 21 meet, I'll explain how every single transaction, no matter how big or small, is a financial transaction. Thus, every single transaction must be handled with the dignity and extreme privacy of a banking transaction, never leaving or escaping the bank vault.

With this in mind, nothing about a user will ever be bought or sold.

The massive privacy concerns I'm currently watching in our large tech providers is morally reprehensible. It's so gross it must be stopped. It can't and won't stop with legislation, no matter how well thought out the new law.

It is akin to selling off all of our private parts to the highest bidder, without a user fully understanding the total ramifications of using a tech service. It plays on the unsuspecting, desperate desire to be liked in unwitting exchange for our most intimate personal moments.

The only way to stop these diabolical practices is to launch a new digital service on the internet, which is so powerful everyone chooses to use it. Pongo is the moral solution to this most desperate problem.

Pongo also has the ability for these large tech companies to become plug and play users themselves of Pongo, to allow their customers to utilize their digital service, without compromising the privacy of the Pongo Vault.

I want Twitter to be part of the 21 Pongo Launch Engine companies to help build the Pongo system, so Twitter as a corporate user pays Pongo $2 a month to run Twitter in a safe, secure manner without compromising the integrity of a Pongo user. I believe Twitter would make more money running Twitter on Pongo than @Jack would make running Twitter on Twitter. That's the objective. @Jack could run Twitter on Pongo and Twitter Classic. Twitter users would likely choose to use Twitter on Pongo, because they would make money from using Twitter, finally.

I believe my Pongo PayOut System is so powerful that @Jack would bring in other tech companies to become corporate users of Pongo for $2 per month to run their services, because everyone would make more money using Pongo than they currently are earning by selling all of our private parts to the highest bidder.

The world needs Pongo, because the world needs to exist in a safe, secure environment.

The only way to make that happen is to build an entire start to finish, big to small Engine where everything stays safely and securely inside a Pongo Bank Vault, treated with the dignity and privacy of a safe banking transaction.

Once Pongo experiences its exponential growth, it's possible the Pongo Bank would be handling more transactions on a larger scale than most other banks. Pongo may turn into one of the world's biggest banks.

I don't know much of anything about the banking industry, especially the process of setting up a bank. It will be imperative that I have a bank mentor, such as Mechanics Bank, located down in the Silicon Valley area, to intimately help me with this process. That's why Mechanics Bank is one of my prospective Founding 21 Pongo Launch Engine entities. I need them to step me through this process.

16

The CES Showfloor Dynamics Change When Pongo is Launched

" MOST DEVICES OPERATING ON PONGO WILL BE ABLE TO BE *"*
GIVEN AWAY FOR FREE IN EXCHANGE FOR THE PONGO USAGE
REVENUE STREAM. YES, DEVICES INCLUDE CARS AND TRUCKS.

With my Pongo vision in mind I attended CES -- the Consumer Electronics Show is the world's largest and most influential tech extravaganza -- to see the scope of connecting every device to Pongo, according to my mission statement.

Connecting every device is a big project. Long after Pongo is in every language, which is years away, Pongo will still be connecting to new devices. Once we have connected to all existing devices, another CES comes around with even more new devices created. This piece of our mission statement is ongoing and will not end. We will always have new devices to connect to new people. Our growth won't stop.

The one aspect which struck me at CES was that very few, almost none, of the devices earn a revenue stream from usage. That hasn't changed. Here we are in 2021 and still few devices earn cash from being used for its specific function.

The flat screen smart TV manufacturer in my living room does not earn an income from my usage of that TV when I watch NFL football. Why not? It's all digital in 2021.

A Ford vehicle is a device. Ford is now thinking in terms of revenue from the use of its online digital services. I'm suspicious, however, that Ford isn't contemplating the potential revenue stream from device usage which would allow it to give away a rig, in exchange for a $2 per month Pongo usage agreement. Yes, I know it sounds crazy. Let's explore it.

How many would opt for buying a Tesla or a Ford, if they could make constant money just from driving a Tesla or a Ford? I put tremendous mileage on my vehicle. I could likely pay a monthly vehicle payment and my large fuel bill from using Pongo while driving.

Pongo won't need to go create the systems to allow each individual device to operate and feed off the Pongo PayOut System. The PayOut will be great enough that the device manufacturers will want to develop the connection to be used by Pongo users, so they can participate in the revenue stream.

It is at this point, the dynamics begin to change on the CES showroom floor.

Most devices operating on Pongo will be able to be given away for free in exchange for the Pongo usage revenue stream. If we can create Pongo so that this can happen for an expensive automobile, we can do it with nearly every device. I want to see Mr. Musk's StarLink satellites available to Pongo users for free, because the revenue stream from the Pongo PayOut System far exceeds what StarLink can generate through its own subscription cost.

The same goes with a Verizon phone. Get a smartphone for free with a $2 per month Pongo subscription. A phone running Pongo should generate more cash for Verizon than Verizon is currently making from the sale and monthly service of their current plans.

The same is true for servers at Oracle. Rather than renting server space to Pongo, I want the servers to generate an income which far exceeds that rent, by grabbing cash from the usage through the Pongo Pay-Out.

This methodology would drive devices to Pongo. We don't have to seek the devices, the device will find and connect to us. The device manufacturers will want the revenue stream.

17

One Dimensional Schizophrenia

" THE FLAT ONE DIMENSIONAL SCHIZOPHRENIA COMES FROM "
TAKING THE OLD CORPORATE STRUCTURE -- A BRICK AND MOR-
TAR MODEL -- AND PLACING THAT OLD STRUCTURE ON TOP OF
THE NEWFANGLED INTERNET.

Considering we have the most genius minds in the world creating our technology companies, I find it odd that pretty much every tech offering is a flat one dimensional platform providing the paying public mere flat one dimensional solutions.

In 2021, we live in a multidimensional world, yet the bulk of the technology we use is flat. It's one dimensional. Still, to this day.

I am not a medical or psychological doctor, nor have I ever played one on TV, such that I am unqualified to give an actual medical diagnosis. With that disclaimer, our technology companies are plagued by schizophrenia. The bigger they get, the more schizophrenic they become.

As much as I would love to talk smack about Bezos and his company, Rainforest is an excellent example of a multidimensional business approach to numerous one dimensional business applications. I surmise it is a primary reason for his tremendous success. In the same manner, every enterprise Elon Musk is involved with is a multidimensional business approach and solution. Thus, I know both Bezos and Musk are multidimensional thinkers and business leaders. They are shining examples, with spectacular success.

Pongo is not one dimensional. Look at Pongo as a sphere -- a multidimensional engine which brings an entire solution. Remember Pongo's Mission Statement, The World's Largest Communications Network Connecting Every Device for Every Person in Every Language Everywhere on Earth. That mission statement can't be fulfilled with a one dimensional offering, nor can it be schizophrenic to be successful. When the mission is ultimately achieved, a user shouldn't need to leave Pongo, nor will they want to.

Let's analyze social media and streaming services, as an example.

The basic premise of social media is to build a tech company where people can upload a photo or video of a cat and people can like or share the photo/video of the cat. That is a flat one dimensional offering. Some social media companies add an additional flat one dimensional offering by allowing people to send each other a private message about their cat. That social media company now has two flat one dimensional offerings. Wowser. A massive social media company will collect a bunch of flat one dimensional offerings, making it appear they are super-duper big with lots of stuff to do. Users are forced to hop from a flat one dimensional offering to another. To use the Smoogle-Boogle or Bluebookey-Facey Thing services they've built or acquired, requires a bunch of hopping and jumping from one platform to another, with each barely connected to each other.

They put all of their one dimensional offerings in a box, hoping it looks multidimensional, but it's just a box with various one dimensional platforms.

The flat one dimensional company collects and sells the user's intimate preferences for cats to make money.

When new social media companies are introduced, however, they are merely carving out a small targeted segment of the population and offering them a smaller flat one dimensional social media service, where their pictures of cats are targeting a small like-minded group of similar cat picture lovers, who don't want to be offended by people sharing cats they don't like and agree with. It's still a flat one dimensional offering, with like-minded cat lovers. No offense to my two beloved cats.

Similarly, streaming services are popping up left and right. Everyone wants to have a streaming service these days and everyone believes their streaming service offerings have a tremendous value, based on the combined content streamed.

Streaming services are also classic flat one dimensional offerings, albeit with different content streaming in each. A streaming service is a place where a company such as Fox or Paramount, put all of their stuff in a streaming service and offer to the public their stuff to watch for a monthly fee. In all actuality, streaming services are flat one dimensional.

We now have huge streaming services which kicked it off, such as BicTheNet. They have lots of stuff from a bunch of folks.

Now, in the same manner as upstart social media, we are seeing smaller targeted streaming services launch, as a special spot for like-minded similar viewers. These are being broken down to market segments based on political beliefs, cultural likenesses, locations and nationalities, genre and interest types. They are all the same formula, the same corporate structure and business model. Many are tremendously successful, because there are enough like-minded folks to pay for their unique streaming service catering to their specific mores. All of these streaming services are still a flat one dimensional offering to the paying public.

The schizophrenia really kicks in when big flat one dimensional companies acquire another flat one dimensional company and combine the two together, pretending as if they are one. The more acquisitions, the more schizophrenic they become.

Each of these acquired companies has its own culture and unique customer base for service. Rarely are they the same as the others. One has foosball machines for their employees, the other has a bowling alley to let go of the stress of the high tech world. The foosballers don't like to play with the bowlers and they wear different shoes. Upper corporate management puts out edicts which demand that everyone must wear the same shoes, for corporate unity sake. That's when corporate schizophrenia becomes apparent. Foosballeres revolt. Bowlers revolt. None of them want to lose their paycheck, yet none of them want to get along. Inevitably, everyone hates the corporate management unified shoe choice.

Of course, this is a tremendously simplistic example. Yet, if one looks at the big picture of corporate acquisitions, this is ultimately one of the big dilemmas.

Pongo will never acquire another company. Such is the antithesis of the Pongo corporate structure, with the Pongo Engine.

As I will lay out for you, Pongo has a different formula. We aren't doing a paradigm shift of how we've done it in the past. We are creating an entirely new corporate structure.

The flat one dimensional schizophrenia comes from taking the old corporate structure -- a brick and mortar model -- and placing that old structure on top of the new fandangled internet.

I've watched this happen from the inception of the tech industry. This became exacerbated once we all went hardcore digital on the internet.

The internet wasn't built for brick and mortar, it's a new structure all together. Thus, a brick and mortar structure and corporate mentality isn't created as the ideal application for internet use. It becomes worse when a long standing brick and mortar company tries to transform or transition to the internet. They weren't made for each other. The result is corporate schizophrenia.

I have created the Pongo structure -- literally how the corporation will function -- to take advantage of the internet. Pongo is not a brick and mortar corporation and never will be. Pongo, unlike all other digital and internet companies, is designed to harness the full power and unique business opportunity of the internet.

The full potential of the internet has never been realized, because no company has been created to specifically harness the massive powerful potential of the internet. Yes, I thought of Smoogle-Boogle when I wrote that sentence.

So far, our world has taken a brick and mortar corporate structure, laid it out on top of the internet and told it "Go ye, brick and mortar, and internetize."

Brick and mortar can't internetize to its full potential.

This isn't a paradigm shift. We are shattering the paradigm and building a new enterprise, designed to harness the digital world. Pongo will revolutionize the internet and all things digital. The problem with brick and mortar? Those dang walls.

18

Tear Down The Walls

" PONGO WILL BE THE FIRST DIGITAL COMPANY WITHOUT "
WALLS. PONGO WILL REVOLUTIONIZE THE DIGITAL LANDSCAPE.
PONGO WILL REDEFINE DIGITAL COMMUNICATIONS.

Let's go on a helicopter ride.

We can get the big picture and understand the current state of affairs, by hopping into a helicopter together to get a different perspective.

This is actually a healthy exercise for any corporate manager or administrator. Take a helicopter ride.

Years ago, I expressed to my corporate computer sales boss, Mike McShane, my frustration about what I was experiencing on the ground in reality of the business transactions and problems I was facing directly. I was telling him about my on-the-street issues.

"Go get in a helicopter and take a ride," Mike told me.

"I don't have a helicopter and you're not paying me enough to buy one."

"Come with me, let's go on a helicopter ride," Mike responded.

He marched me out of the office to change the scenery. Out in the parking lot, I looked around for my helicopter. Nothing flashy, swooshy and big caught my eye.

"I don't understand," I told him, somewhat annoyed. He was wasting my time. I had sales to make, commission to grab.

"Daniel, you just told me about your perspective on the ground. I want you to get up in the air, look down on it all and tell me what you are seeing happen in the big picture, from above it all."

"Oh, I can do that."

As we walked around the parking lot, I described what I could view from the air. All of the on-the-ground circumstances changed in perspective from the air, as I could see all the pieces and parts interacting together. Everything on the ground began to make sense, as I saw it all as a whole working together and not.

"Now, watch yourself down there and carefully tell me how you are seeing yourself play your role in the big picture," Mike instructed.

I described the perceived dysfunction around me which caused me frustration on the ground and how I was reacting to it.

From our helicopter, we saw what needed to change, what needed to be made better, how everything would function smoothly and perfectly, according to everything else we watched.

It was one of the most fascinating rides I've ever taken in my life. It was all about perspective.

Let's take a helicopter ride together.

Let's look down on the digital internet industry as a whole, the big picture.

To give it some real perspective, let's look at specific digitally based internet companies. Let's look at some of the 21 companies I'm wanting to be part of the Pongo engine launch.

From above, up high, looking out across the world from our super-duper big helicopter, what's the first odd piece you notice?

All of those dang walls. Everyone has walls. We're all walled off.

There's Verizon. Their walls are big -- massive expansive walls. The walls are funky shaped, because the walls kept expanding and growing every time Verizon acquired a new company, but everything is within those Verizon walls.

As broad and expansive as their walls, Verizon can't go beyond those walls. Their walls contain it.

Other companies have built their walls close to Verizon. They want their folks and the Verizonites to be able to go back and forth, so they build a little tunnel to handle the traffic. Yet, still, it's limited by walls.

These are the brick and mortar walls.

Next we see Procter & Gamble. Wow, impressive walls. There's someone running with a box of Tide. Kaboom. They hit the wall. The box of Tide can't go further. The box of Tide is stuck in the P&G walls, unless it gets on a specific truck traveling through a contracted tunnel heading over to the Kroger walls.

To get there, it stops at walls of a specifically selected contracted warehouse. The Tide hangs out in those walls for a bit.

It hops on another truck, going through a specific tunnel dictated by the wall agreement to make its way to Kroger.

Within the Kroger walls the box of Tide flies around Kroger, but can't leave those walls.

It's limited by the walls.

We are watching the digital "walled" transactions happening before our eyes, involving physical products moving between brick and mortar walls.

As our helicopter hovers, look over there. The same thing is happening in the digital walls of the NFL.

Notice how CBS and Fox have their walls set up nearby, so the digital NFL game can break out of the digital walled stadium and go through the specific contracted tunnel only leading to digital walls of CBS or Fox.

The digital NFL, can't leave the digital walls of CBS and Fox. It's stuck there, by contract. The walls won't let it escape.

The digital, contracted NFL walls are to protect the NFL content. The walls of protection also contain and restrain the content.

From our perspective in the air, we can see all of the expansive space around the world, where the digital NFL can go, yet, we also see that the vast majority of the world can't get into the NFL walls. Yes, the digital walls of NFL, CBS and Fox are big and go all over, yet, in the big picture, the digital NFL content still isn't reaching the power and potential of the massive digital internet going around the world.

Why? Because the NFL can't make money outside of its walls, using its current brick and mortar corporate structure it is utilizing on the internet.

Now, look through that window of our 'copter. Those are the Ford walls. You see the same thing happening. The Ford F-250 leaves the Ford walls and goes through the tunnel to the Ford dealership walls.

The Ford dealership has a blow up floppy thing inside its walls to attract a customer's attention. It sets up a megaphone from the wall to tell customers "come into our walls, it's the only way you can get this Ford F-250 you really want."

Our physical products and services are stuck inside digital brick and mortar walls.

From this perspective, while we are using this expensive helicopter for a ride, look down around the world and find Pongo's walls.

What? What are you telling me that you can't find the Pongo walls? There must be walls. Everybody has walls.

What do you mean, Pongo doesn't have walls?

How can a company function without walls? It's a brick and mortar must.

Pongo will be the first digital company without walls.

Pongo will revolutionize the digital landscape. Pongo will redefine digital communications.

Why?

Because, I have a formula to pay for it all. People will actually make money using the internet -- everyone will. It's the power and potential of the internet. It's what the internet was created to do. Pongo will harness the internet for the first time, for every person on earth. That's our mission.

We will be able to do this, because Pongo doesn't have walls, it reaches everywhere on earth.

I believe Sir Tim Berners-Lee understands this.

DANIEL WEBSTER

19

The Pongo Vision Replaced My Newspaper

" IT DIDN'T TAKE ME TOO LONG TO REALIZE THAT I HAD JUST "
BOUGHT A BUSINESS WHICH HAD A DECISIVE END POINT. THE
NEW FANDANGLED INTERNET WAS GOING TO KILL MY NEWSPA-
PER. MY NEWSPAPER DIED. IT'S TIME FOR PONGO TO COME
ALIVE.

I began this journey by heading off to college to learn how to program mainframe computers -- in the early 1980s.

To be frank, I believe the phone I'm typing on right now may have more computing power than the mainframe I wanted to code.

After a year of heat at DeVry University in Phoenix, Ariz., I decided I needed music in my life, in addition to coding. I transferred to Biola University in Southern California.

By chance, I happened to be working a part time job at the Biola Bookstore when a startup Fruit company picked Biola University to be one of its original ten test locations to sell its new personal computer, the M Box, to college students.

It was an absolutely brilliant move for the Fruit company. It began putting their computer brand into the hands of students who would ultimately enter the workforce and change the computing brand loyalty at many employers.

When I first began selling the M Box, I didn't actually have the M Box to show the students. I had brochures and a massive, heavy Lisa, the M Box predecessor.

I explained that their M Box would be about half the size of the Lisa on my desk. There was a carrying case available. They could carry their computer around.

I explained and showed them pictures how it had two floppy drives, but the disk didn't actually flop. I tried to sell them on an external 10 meg hard drive. Every student would ask "how many pages would I have to type to fill up a 10 meg hard drive?"

"A bunch," I would respond. "You probably won't ever type that many pages, but, you can do drawings in this program. Drawings and graphics take up a lot more disk space."

"I'll never use it to draw pictures. I'm just going to type."

"Oh, but everyone is going to do pictures and graphics. Just watch, you'll see," I said from my small corner in the back of the bookstore.

I sold a slew of M Boxes from my back corner.

I've been involved in this industry for a long while. I've watched and analyzed intimately. Later, in corporate computer sales, I rode the aerospace industry.

Before Sir Tim Berners-Lee launched his World Wide Web, my employer was one of the companies which launched Prodigy. It was a group of large corporations which came together to build a new communications network, we would ultimately understand as the internet concept. There was an obligation for me to convince people to use this new dial up Prodigy system to read news, send messages, purchase plane tickets and buy stocks.

I was faced with "but, I'd rather call someone up on the phone than send a message -- it's faster."

"Oh, but everyone will be doing it soon," I'd respond.

"But, I like to go look through the brochures at my travel agency. My travel agent is so friendly and helpful," they'd tell me.

"But, I like to call my stock broker when I want to buy. My broker takes me golfing every two years," was a good excuse to not use Prodigy to buy stocks.

"Oh, but everyone will be doing it soon," seemed to be my standard answer.

I was personally responsible for gutting the profit margins of personal computer sales, as I knew I could make up my commission check in volume by selling thousands of PCs a month by beating everyone's price. I personally took profit margins down from 18 to 25 percent to a mere few points. The entire industry was forced to ultimately adjust its commission schedules based on my gutter price points.

I loved selling to aerospace. They needed thousands of the newest, fastest, most powerful computers every month. They had to replace nearly every machine when I sold the first 1 gig computer. It was marvelous and lucrative.

I was out visiting my biggest aerospace customer in El Segundo, when the head of corporate procurement dropped the bomb.

"All corporate procurements have been stopped," she told me.

Something happened in Washington D.C. which stopped my paycheck.

I needed to broaden my customer base.

I came up with a creative idea and thought about Wycliffe Bible Translators, located in Huntington Beach at the time.

I took out a new portable Compaq computer for a sales call with their two-person Wycliffe technology team. It had a rechargeable battery pack.

I tried to convince them that every Bible translator around the world needed to have a portable computer. When they got to a phone line where they were translating, they could dial in and send their translations to headquarters.

"But, we have this big mainframe."

They showed me the mainframe. It was indeed a Cray mainframe. The same Cray mainframe I learned to program at DeVry.

They couldn't conceive of needing one of those portable personal computers with a battery pack. Years later, I would read a feature article in the Los Angeles Times about Wycliffe equipping all of their translators with laptop computers to do translation work in the field. Someone else earned the commission from that sale.

After receiving my Juris Doctor in law school, I moved back to my hometown and bought my local small-town weekly newspaper in 1998. I had sweet-talked my way into the position as interim editor of my future competition, so the corporate owned daily newspaper would teach me local journalism before I bought my weekly.

It didn't take me too long to realize that I had just bought a business which had a decisive end point. The new fandangled internet, known as Tim BL's World Wide Web, was going to kill my newspaper.

In fact, if I created a website, I would destroy it myself faster.

It wasn't just a problem I faced. It was the dilemma of every newspaper, big or small, around the world. I was not alone.

The massive problem, the revenue stream from a website could not possibly support a local news service, big or small.

I knew a newspaper and a website could not coexist successfully together. It was one or the other, and Tim BL was going to win.

I had to come up with an internet solution to save my newspaper and successfully support a local news service.

As I analyzed where my revenue was coming from, an internet solution had to bring the cash to my community, as my newspaper was producing from the biggest to the smallest revenue sources.

A local news internet solution had to be able to pluck revenue from the biggest, tallest tree, while serving the local businesses which I served successfully with my local paper. Corporate co-op advertising dollars were a large cash flow through the corporate newspaper inserts. The local restaurant and hair salon was absolutely dependent on me to get their paid messages out to their small community. I needed both to survive.

A digital internet solution had to feed from both those revenue streams.

Here we are in 2021 and we still don't have that solution. We still don't have a successful online solution to make that happen. We need a turnkey system to turn on to save our local news sources. Pongo is coming, my friend. The time to launch is now.

I also knew that when I went digital, my newspaper had to transform to a live video solution. Thus, Pongo had to go live, via video.

The Pongo solution had to broadcast live video from my local small-town high school football field.

The problem with live video, at the time in my neck of the woods, was I was making phone calls on Verizon 1X towers. I couldn't go live from my high school football field via 1X and most of my readers were still dialing up to get online.

My friend Mark Hash was selling TV satellites at the time for my former aerospace customer in El Segundo and began offering their new internet satellite. I asked Mark if I could broadcast a live football game by setting up one of his satellites on the sidelines. It wasn't possible using basic upload speed -- equivalent to dial-up -- at the time. So much for that idea.

Technology wasn't ready for Pongo. Technology hadn't been created yet and brought to my community.

Once the vision for Pongo came to me in its fullness, the harsh reality hit.

Pongo is so big, I can't afford to build it for my small community. In order to create a system for a successful small news service like mine, the cost to build it would be so outlandish, a small news service could never recoup the cost.

In order to build it, Pongo had to be built for the entire world, making it available as the digital solution for all local news sources, big or small -- just so my small-town could have its digital news system.

The other funky issue I encountered with Pongo was it would be ludicrous to build an entire massive system from scratch when someone else would build the pieces and parts. There's no point in recreating the wheel.

I had the formula and system, those who built the actual technology would need to all come together to join me to put it all into one cohesive, complete system -- once they finally built the pieces and parts.

Building Pongo would be similar to the corporate collaborative effort that built Prodigy in the 1980s, yet the timing had to be right this time.

For this to happen, everybody had to make cash off the system. Everybody is everybody, not just the super-big special everybodies.

I've been waiting for the world to build all my technology pieces and parts. The world has finally created it all. Now, the corporations with the world's technology will hopefully hook up with me, the guy with the formula to put it all together in a financially successful manner.

I'm not one of the tech gurus which have launched so many other technology companies. I am the one with the formula to build it all out in a financially successful manner to make it a business opportunity available for everyone.

I'm a small-town newspaper publisher who, out of desperation, came up with the solution to save the world's news industry. Now, it's time to connect everyone together. Because, when we save the news industry, we save the internet.

If you know or have connections with any of the presidents and CEOs of the 21 companies I mention by name in this crowdsourcing business plan, would you please contact them for me and tell them that Daniel Webster is trying to reach them. I don't need their cash, I need their technology in exchange for a licensing royalty agreement to make their cash from my formula.

Of course, as you've noticed with the missing chapters, I'm not going to tell you my specific patent pending formula here in this book. I will do that when all 21 of us get together to discuss this matter further.

20

No, I'm Not Looking for Cash -- Right Now

" IF I HAVE AN AGREEMENT WITH THESE 21 COMPANIES, I "
WOULD HAVE CASH POUNDING ON MY DOOR BEGGING TO BE IN-
VOLVED.

It's typically the first "WAT" I get when I talk about Pongo.

It defies everything we do when we launch a start-up these days. First stop is always a heavy hitter venture capital firm. Everybody knows that. After all, the notion of crowdsourcing alone is typically to generate start-up cash.

Going to seek venture capital cash is actually backwards for Pongo. Remember, Pongo isn't a normal start-up, as we aren't creating a typical tech business. We are rebuilding the internet, correctly this time.

The first step in this Pongo process is to bring 21 companies -- families of technology -- to come together just to consider, explore, pursue and ultimately agree to put their technologies into a massive quilting bee to sew it all together in one, complete, cohesive engine which will expand and continue to grow, until it becomes the world's largest communications network connecting every device for every person in every language everywhere on earth.

It really doesn't cost me anything to connect with these 21 companies. I just need the president and CEO of each of them to know that I am trying to connect with them. Connecting with the 21 is cheap --

it involves a tenacious, creative spirit. The need for cash comes after I know I have an agreement with these companies.

If I have an agreement with these 21 companies, I would have cash pounding on my door begging to be involved.

Quibyebye proved that having $1.7 billion in cash doesn't actually make a viable business plan and formula.

I don't want to prove that I can be my own dot com bubble bust. I want the most genius minds in 21 companies to flush out, approach Pongo with a hyper-critical manner, analyze every tiny aspect and nuance of Pongo to make sure that everything is perfect before launch, so billions of dollars isn't blown up at launch.

I want the greatest legal minds, making sure that I have indeed created a company which will never become a monopoly and never subjected to antitrust laws -- as I believe I have created.

I want those who have built massive networks to go through Pongo with a fine tooth comb to make sure it will indeed operate as a smooth, cohesive engine capable of operating worldwide without walls.

21

Gaming will be a Cash Cow

" THE BRILLIANT MINDS AT ACTIVISION BLIZZARD WILL PUSH "
THE TECHNOLOGY OF PONGO FURTHER THAN PROBABLY ANY
OTHER PONGO USAGE AND APPLICATION.

When all's said and done, gaming will prove to be one of Pongo's big cash cows. Which is why I'm inviting Activision Blizzard to be a member of my Founding 21.

Why?

Because gamers love hanging out in a digital system for hours, doing what they love to do most. With Pongo, gamers and their gaming manufacturers could make a ton of cash simply hanging out on the couch doing what they love to do most.

I don't have hand to eye coordination. Entire teams cry when I play baseball. I learned early on, there's no point in intentionally subjecting myself to humiliation. Thus, I personally am not a gamer. It's frustrating and embarrassing, for everyone involved.

The folks at Activision Blizzard are gaming folks. They know their market and users brilliantly.

The genius minds at Activision Blizzard can take my Pongo Engine and PayOut System to Happily, Highly Monetize their gaming world to turn Pongo into the dominant gaming platform.

The minds in Santa Monica will push the technology of Pongo further than probably any other Pongo usage and application.

By making gaming a primary function of Pongo, all other aspects of Pongo will be pushed technologically further.

Gaming will push Pongo to where we're going, rather than developing for where we are or where we've been. Gaming will drive Pongo to achieve the future, right now. I don't need hand to eye coordination to know that.

I look forward to exploring how gaming will interact with a Happily, Highly Monetized system, without intruding on a gaming experience. I look forward to the Activision Blizzard pieces and parts.

For the sake of a gamer and all other members of the Founding 21, Pongo must be a native gaming platform.

22

The Pongo Experience

"WE WERE CREATED TO TOUCH, FEEL AND PHYSICALLY CONNECT WITH OTHER PEOPLE. PONGO TRANSFORMS LIVES BY RECONNECTING PEOPLE TO THEIR COMMUNITY THROUGH WHAT THEY DO, WHERE THEY LIVE, WHAT THEY CARE ABOUT. AND EVERYONE MAKES CASH."

I don't have a demo to show you how Pongo works to give you a feeling of the experience. In order to make a demo, I'd need to bring together 21 Pongo Launch Engine companies to build it. When that happens, we won't be building a demo, we'll build Pongo.

Therefore, I am limited to describing for you in textual form my demo.

Furthermore, my interactive simple Pongo shell for the content and monetization is part of my secret patent pending special sauce. Wink.

World Premiere Movie Night

I can't wait for the first world premiere of a movie in a theater running Pongo.

Yes, there will be specific movie theaters which will opt to use their digital equipment to run a Pongo equipped live movie experience for Pongo users. A movie theater is simply another place for digital devices which all need to connect to Pongo. The live interactive user experience would be dynamic and preferred by many.

As the movie stars make their way down the red carpet, I'm not waiting for the photos to hit the tabloids the next day, as I am participating in it all live as it happens. My favorite media sites are all broadcasting it on Pongo. I'm literally joining the chorus of fans around the world from my living room, as I fawn with lavish praise the fab-u-lous dress my superstar is wearing. She looks gor-ge-ous.

I'm inviting my friends to join me at the Paramount movie premiere, so we can group-fawn together. I'm happily making money doing this, just by doing it. The superstar headliner is giddy with all the previously untapped cash pouring into her Pongo Bank Vault, just for being fab-u-lous and having millions of people around the world showing up to her movie premiere. The superstar is making Paramount happy, as they are making more cash.

Before the movie starts, she interacts with fans on Pongo, knowing every interaction at a world premiere generates an amazing amount of additional cash. Paramount encourages her to do it, maybe even by contract, so the studio is generating even more never-before-realized cash.

As the lights of the Pongo equipped theater dim, all the Pongo devices in the house automatically go into unobtrusive Pongo Theater Mode.

Verizon personal devices are running in perfect synchronicity with the move screen. Personal monetization is happening constantly as the movie plays. The income didn't end with $17.69 at the door and $19.40 at the concession stand. Furthermore, a Pongo premiere extends the experience to millions at home.

Because our eyes and reactions have become so multi-task oriented, we are already accustomed to processing many visual elements at once. It's no longer strange, in fact, for many in younger generations, it's preferred to be in Pongo Theater Mode. They will do it at home, as well as the theater.

The superstar knows when moments are coming up in the movie when she will need to have a big personal reaction to what she sees, because she knows the millions of fans will react by pouring more cash into her Vault, as they react too.

As the superstar's real time PayOut Cash Counter grows, her fans push it harder, being driven to make her rank as the richest movie premiere superstar in history. We are no longer defined by likes and follows, we are defined by the amount of cash from Pongo PayOut going through the Pongo Bank Vault.

Mind you, users at home are already doing all of these pieces and parts while they're watching a movie -- they just aren't pushing cash through a system constantly as they do it. With Pongo, everybody makes money. Our superstar will make a bunch of cash. The new studio contracts after Pongo's launch will likely be structured accordingly, because it's smart business for the studio. Paramount will make more money by using my Pongo formula.

And everyone will have a fabulous time.

High School Football Truck Night in America

If I were a betting man, I'd bet that once Pongo is rolling, there will be one particular Friday Night which will kick Black Friday's butt.

More cash will be generated that night than Black Friday has ever seen. It will break all single day sales totals, and fund our high school sports programs across America at the same time.

Truck Night in America happens when all the high schools across the nation decide that on one particular Friday night everybody should buy a Ford or Tesla truck, during the live local high school football game broadcasting on Pongo.

Remember, commissions and royalties are paid out to the content creators, including everyone involved. Thus, a local high school football program is the talent creating the content, in the same manner NFL is the talent in a NFL stadium. A high school football field, for the Pongo system, is simply a smaller stadium.

There are nearly 16,000 high school football teams in the United States. Crazy Math: If we can get half the high school football teams broadcasting their Friday Night Football game on Pongo, with a small average of 1,000 fans participating on Pongo, and convince only five percent of the fans to buy the truck or car they were thinking of buying, planning to buy or sweet talked into buying during the Truck Night in America Friday Night as a fundraiser for their high school, at an average truck price of $50,000, Pongo would push through $20,000,000,000 in truck sales in one night, with a chunk of the proceeds going to the school in commission and royalty from the Pongo PayOut System. $8,000 \times 1,000 \times .05 \times 50,000 = \$20$ billion in vehicle sales in one night beats Black Friday revenue.

Yes, it's crazy math and, yes, it could happen. It's the power of local support for local news and local sports, combined with the potential buying power of people purchasing what they would be buying otherwise and funneling commissions and royalties to a content creator network.

The beautiful aspect of Pongo will be its intuitive push for sales. Think about Pongo connecting all of the processes from Ford, through distribution and warehousing, down to the dealer level delivering the Ford truck. It won't take the Pongo algorithm long to intuitively be able to in advance of Truck Night in America notify Ford of how many specific new vehicles, with which features and colors, it needs to pre-deliver to specific high school football stadiums, based on the anticipated audience size, response, and anticipated sales. New truck owners could take delivery and drive home from the football game in their new rig. Many people will pre-order their new vehicle, for purchase during the game.

Why do you think I want ViacomCBS involved with the Pongo Launch Engine? In my view, yes, Paramount and CBS are powerful assets to help Pongo build out. MaxPreps, however, is the perfect, strategically brilliant, launch partner for Pongo's high school sports. Pongo needs MaxPreps and MaxPreps needs Pongo.

Once the public begins to fully understand the concept, they will pre-order their weekly Kroger grocery shopping, so Kroger receives the order during their local football game. Users will begin to shop according to their royalties and commissions going to their other favorite events or TV shows.

23

What Laws Apply: Is Pongo a Tech Company, Public Utility, Social Media, Streaming Service or What?

> " IN REALITY, PONGO IS A BANK. EVERY TRANSACTION IN PONGO " IS A FINANCIAL TRANSACTION, EVEN IF IT'S FOR A SMALL FRACTION OF A PENNY. THUS, EVERY TRANSACTION MUST BE KEPT PRIVATE AND NEVER LEAVE THE PONGO BANK VAULT.

None of the above.

I'm not so sure we've defined what Pongo is, such that we aren't sure which laws apply.

Watching congressional hearings in Washington, D.C. with technology company executives is embarrassing. I'm literally embarrassed for the members of the House and Senate. Their ignorance of basic technology is stunning -- it's on full public display. They actually don't have a clue what they are talking about. But, we keep electing them, so there you have it. I applaud @Jack and Mark for sitting cold-faced while patiently answering the questions.

The actual real life problem which comes glaring out during these hearings is that people who don't have a clue are creating laws they know nothing about.

I've noticed that few in Washington D.C. truly think. They flatout don't think and reason. I, of course, use broad brush strokes to paint that picture. There are some in Washington for whom I have tremendous respect. They've earned it.

That's our system. That's how we do things. We live with what we've got.

The conundrum for Pongo: which laws apply?

Philosophically, Pongo would be under legal standards as a tech company, with tech company laws applying to our business practices.

According to how we handle users' communications, Pongo will treat them as a phone company, a public utility.

In reality, Pongo is a bank.

Every transaction on Pongo is a financial transaction, even if it's for a small fraction of a penny. Thus, every transaction must be kept private and never leave the Pongo Bank Vault.

Pongo will hold itself to such a high standard of safety, security and confidentiality that laws -- no matter what section of the legal code -- won't touch us. We will be the most trusted bank, the most trusted public utility, the most trusted social media, the most trusted streaming service, the most trusted tech company in the world -- all to protect our users and their personal and private information and communications.

We will hold ourselves to such a high standard, laws created by clueless ding-dongs won't touch us.

Considering how our Pongo business strategy and mission statement is structured, to preserve its integrity, we must take such an approach.

Nothing leaves the Vault.

Nobody can buy information from the Vault, nobody has access to the Vault.

If law enforcement needs something from the Vault, Pongo will respond to a judge's signature on a search warrant. It's the law.

It's nobody's business what a user watches and which advertisers have messages to which user. That's personal, confidential information.

Every ad is designed for me and you as an individual Pongo user. The Pongo formula chooses confidentially which ad I view. Only Pongo knows what I do with that advertisement.

Advertisers, marketers, manufacturers which want access to Pongo users, can't directly reach them. They must go to Pongo, and Pongo will reach them on their behalf, using our internal algorithm.

That being stated, Pongo also will provide companies the richest, deepest, market tools to tailor and allow the companies to sell more effectively than ever before. Pongo is driven by sales of products and services. Pongo will help businesses sell.

Pongo ultimately makes its biggest cash from selling. We will help companies sell, intuitively. We will help companies stock inventory, intuitively.

Conceivable, as the Pongo algorithm learns more and more, faster and faster, someone with a large, empty warehouse or a store seeking to serve a small community, can turn on Pongo for $2 per month and have Pongo tell them the amount of specific items to have in stock on a particular day, to deliver to their customer base that day. Pongo will seek to squeeze days in inventory and turn a company's inventory quickly. Pongo will know our communities and intimately understand our customers better than anyone else, because of our algorithm. We will be a company's greatest business partner. We will help companies make more profit. If our business users succeed, Pongo succeeds.

Pongo won't build warehouses, Pongo will help a company utilize its warehouse effectively and more profitably.

With the Pongo Engine, everything around the world is working in singular synchronicity. It is similar, however, more encompassing, to what MartInWalls is seeking to achieve with its online shopping experience.

Kroger doesn't have to be solely dependent on its own warehousing and inventory supply, using the Pongo system. Pongo can automatically move merchandise across even various different companies, if a company prefers. Remember, it's all digital, in one cohesive engine, operating in one strategic formula to drive sales for everyone, so the entire network can feed off the cash generated from sales, in the form of royalties and commissions.

Conversely, the power of this massive, powerful Engine will put the capabilities into the hands of the smallest to the biggest. Actual lives will change when given the opportunity and empowerment to succeed.

It's 2021, folks, we can do this. We've created all the pieces and parts. Pongo will put it all together in one Engine.

24

No More Apps, Ever

" APPS ARE OVER, WHEN PONGO LAUNCHES. EVERYONE, ACROSS "
THE BOARD, WILL REALIZE THAT THE ENTIRE APP CONCEPT
WAS A BAD IDEA AND THEY'LL NEVER WANT TO USE A SYSTEM
DEPENDENT ON APPS AGAIN.

Apps are the worst idea ever. I don't fault those who came up with the idea as the solution, as they didn't know better.

Once we understood the downfall and privacy disaster of the app world, we had to come up with a better solution and turn the privacy concerns around.

In the high tech world, we should never say "oh, but, that's how we do things."

That's bull. By definition, technology is about how we should do things and creating systems which do what we must and should do.

Apps are over, when Pongo launches. Everyone, across the board, will realize that the entire app concept was simply a bad, awful idea and they'll never want to use a system dependent on apps again.

Just the annoyance of picking an app is enough to make someone go crazy.

First, I'm depending on a tech company I don't necessarily trust such as Smoogle-Boogle to look after my best interests to make the judgement on what apps I have to choose. By virtue of an app being in the app store, I know that Smoogle-Boogle says it's alright -- the same company which is selling my private parts for cash, because that's their primary founding business plan. Most importantly, I don't really know who the app is truly coming from.

Second, I'm dependent on other users -- some smarter, some dumber than me -- to tell me if I should trust and download an app. They give me stars to look at. They write comments, most worthless. Still, I don't have much security in knowing if I should download the app. I don't know who the app is coming from.

Third, most brutal, I must enter into a new user contract with the app. I'm actually one of the three people who reads the entire contract. I know I'm weird. I have a Juris Doctor. By nature, I must. The user agreement is awful. Nobody should ever agree to a single one of these contracts, however, we don't have a choice. I somewhat joke about selling our private parts to the highest bidder. It's not a joke. We are contracting to do it. The truly perverse part, considering the value of our private information, the tech company is selling our private parts for pennies. Our personal value has been reduced to a penny. And the tech company gets to use the excuse of "you agreed to it in the contract" that we didn't read, couldn't comprehend, didn't understand the ramifications, with someone we don't know or trust.

Fourth, we are giving our credit card and financial information to someone we don't know, don't trust and don't even know where they are located and what they are doing with our private financial information. Considering my extra diligence in choosing which app I download, it fully pisses me off when I, of all people, get duped by an app and have my financial information used inappropriately.

We've been doing this app thing since 2008, with no tech company smart enough to come up with a better, safer, more secure alternative, or so they say. No high tech company should ever say "that's how we do it" for a decade.

We need to kill off the app world and send it to the proverbial dustpan of history. Apps can all hang out with the dead newspapers.

There is a better way. There is hope. Pongo is coming. #GoPongo

The capabilities of Pongo will far exceed the abilities of apps. All of the app makers will turn their former app into a module to the Pongo system, such that they can take advantage of the Pongo PayOut and offer their unique capabilities to the entire network of Pongo users, yet never have access to the Pongo Bank Vault. As with all users, big or small, it will cost $2 per month for a former "apper" to make money from Pongo.

For example, if Smoogle-Boogle really believes that they have the best indexing and search results and wants Pongo users to have the ability to choose a Smoogle-Boogle search because it's their favorite, Smoogle-Boogle can pay Pongo $2 a month to offer their search capabilities to Pongo users. Smoogle-Boogle will make money just by someone telling Pongo to "search Smoogle-Boogle for . . . " Smoogle-Boogle won't have access to the Pongo Vault and won't be able to sell a Pongo user's private information, however, Smoogle-Boogle would likely make more money from running Smoogle-Boogle on Pongo than they ever could make running Smoogle-Boogle on Smoogle-Boogle.

Smoogle-Boogle is so big, powerful and dominant. What makes me so outrageously arrogant to think they would use Pongo, an upstart? Because my formula is superior, my business strategy is better, my Pongo PayOut makes more money. I know the Smoogle-Boogle business formula. I've had to use it. I know how they work. I've had to give them my money. I've watched how their system cashes out. I know how they make their money. Most importantly, I know the cash they are missing.

I created Pongo to blow Smoogle-Boogle out of the water and reduce their dominance, or join my Pongo PayOut formula with the rest of the world.

Plus, Smoogle-Boogle will want access to the capabilities of the entire Pongo Engine. It's worth $2 a month.

The same can be said for Mark's Bluebookey-Facey Thing. I've given Mark a bunch of money. I know his formula. It sucks. I give Mark money, he doesn't give me any. Great for Mark, bad for me, until a new mousetrap is created.

We aren't doing a paradigm shift, moving a paradigm a foot and a half so everyone goes "ooooo, aahhh" at the little shift. We are smashing the paradigm. We are tearing down the walls. We are revolutionizing the internet and online landscape. Pongo is not a brick and mortar company. We won't put brick and mortar on top of the internet and pretend like we're high tech.

For the first time, Pongo will utilize the full power and potential of the internet. They may stop calling it the internet, as it may be called Pongo soon. #GoPongo

There's one person I believe I am insync with regarding my vision for Pongo. I'm not sure everything he has in the mix, however, I've written much of this book for him. It would be a tremendous honor to work with and be mentored by Sir Tim Berners-Lee and his Inrupt. I have a spot in my Founding 21 Pongo Launch Engine companies just for him.

25

The $2 Per Month Pongo Contract is the Most Valuable Asset in the Mix

" WE HAVE A MISSION TO CONNECT EVERYONE, REGARDLESS OF *"* THEIR STANDARD OF LIVING. WHAT WE ARE BUILDING RE- QUIRES A PAID CONTRACT FOR SERVICES. OUR PAID CONTRACT MUST BE AFFORDABLE.

Pongo can't be free. We need an easy to understand paid contract with everyone. Pongo must be affordable for everyone, in every status of life, big or small.

Everyone can afford $2 a month in the U.S. In other monetary systems, Pongo will be priced at the equivalent affordable amount, which may not be a specific $2 U.S. dollar exact exchange. It will be priced at an affordable amount, set according to the living and income standards of the country, such that everyone in that part of the world can afford it. We have a mission to connect everyone, regardless of their standard of living.

Let's use the United States $2 per month for our discussion here. Everyone from the richest to someone on a fixed public assistance income can afford $2 every month. Everyone pays $2 per month.

Small town news content creators will be more dependent on the steady residual income from the $2 per month subscription base they develop. This residual will be the steady stream of income to buy the fuel they need to get to the next high school football game they need to cover. I know.

Why a paid contract? Why not give it away for free?

I want a paid, easy to understand contract between all users and Pongo that dictates how we legally interact with each other. There will be no confusion over the matter, the terms of the contract are so simple and easy to understand, everyone knows in advance what is expected of them.

There's nothing to hide in Pongo. We want everyone to understand, so they get the most out of using Pongo.

The foremost reason for the paid contract is to lock everyone into the exclusive Pongo Arbitration System. Nobody will go to civil court in a legal matter involving any transaction on Pongo. Period. We all agree to use Pongo's Arbitration System.

Our arbitration system applies to all civil matters. It applies to disagreement over content flowing through Pongo. It applies to the products sold on Pongo. It applies to everything. We won't go to civil court on any matter, as the paid Pongo contract will require such.

If I were to guess, Procter & Gamble may prefer to sell a box of Tide through Kroger using exclusively the Pongo Engine, because P&G would prefer to never go to court over any matter involving any product they sell -- not that anyone would ever want to sue over a delightful box of Tide.

For this to happen, the box of Tide must exclusively stay in the Pongo Vault all the way from leaving P&G until it ends up in the customer's laundry room. If the box of Tide leaves the Pongo system along the way, it loses its protection of the Pongo Arbitration System, agreed to in a paid contract.

This is why the Pongo Engine is built to go start to finish, biggest to smallest. Products, services and content should never leave the Pongo Vault and its exclusive Pongo Arbitration System.

This is especially important for the content which flows through the Pongo Engine.

When I first came up with my Pongo vision, I understood that I had to legally protect the companies involved in the Pongo Engine from the content, especially, flowing through the Pongo Engine.

I also have an obligation to legally protect those involved in the Pongo Engine from the products and services advertised and sold through the Pongo Engine.

To do this, nobody gets to go to civil court. Period. For anything.

The Pongo Arbitration System kicks in instantly with any dispute over any matter.

"Fake News"

If someone wants to file a complaint accusing someone of publishing "fake news," the Pongo Arbitration System kicks in and deals with that complaint. The decision is final when the Pongo Arbitration System makes a determination.

To give you an insight into my mindset, as entertaining as I personally find the notion of people screaming "fake news," I find it destructive, as it flies in the face of pure, established journalistic standards.

When I came up with my Pongo Arbitration System, "fake news" hadn't been coined and popularized. I have a firm belief that an allegation of "fake news" must be accompanied by a specific allegation filed within a specific amount of time with documented evidence of why the "news" is "fake." If it's determined that the allegation of "fake news" is correct, the publisher must be given the opportunity to un-fake their news. If it's determined that it isn't "fake news," the "fake news" screamer must shut up.

That's pure journalism.

We all agree to this method in a paid contract.

The concept of legal fairness, righteousness and purity will govern the Pongo Arbitration System. It's only fair.

Psst. Secret.

I think the Pongo Arbitration System itself is worth a mega corporation choosing to use Pongo to handle all of its transactions. It may reduce the budgetary expenditures in their corporate counsel office.

Unliked Content

Pongo must serve every person around the world -- all of them.

Pongo has no bias, bent, political leaning, belief system and is not beholden to any cancel-culture.

Pongo must be a public utility and bank, allowing service to everyone, regardless of who they are and what they think.

Legal standards of free speech change in every country around the world. A country's government can dictate, under their laws, what content is legal in their country using their country's internet lines. Conversely, Pongo has a mission statement to serve every person and Pongo will fulfill that mission.

In order to serve every person in every language everywhere on earth, as our mission dictates, Pongo can't cancel a user. Imagine if Ma Bell listened to our phone calls and turned off our phone service because Ma found a particular private conversation offensive. Ma wouldn't have a Bell -- Ma would lose her business. I'm entirely aware that this analogy is fully missed by several entire generations. LOL.

Thus, the offensive content is determined by the individual hearer of the content. A Pongo user determines offensiveness and Pongo is obligated by its paid contract with a user to prevent that user from ever experiencing offense. Dealing with offense is between an individual user and

Pongo. Pongo adamantly agrees to and has a system to prevent offending a user.

Let me give you an example. There was a tremendously popular "war movie" I had seen in the theater, along with millions of other people who obviously loved the movie. I knew that my father, who hadn't seen it yet, would love to watch it. I turned it on for dad and I to watch in his living room. I didn't pay attention to the rating, I didn't contemplate the content, I only thought about its popularity as a Hollywood blockbuster.

My mother was in the adjoining kitchen.

Shortly after the movie began, the superstar dropped an f-bomb. I didn't think anything of it. Dad didn't react. The word seemed normal in the course of conversation in the movie.

My mother began sobbing in the kitchen and cried "I've avoided hearing that word in my home my entire life and never wanted to ever hear it in my house."

Her offense was real. Such an offense may be mocked in other homes, but, in my house that offense must be taken seriously because it had an obvious, visceral, real reaction to it -- she was sobbing real tears over real pain in her real home.

I was the bad Pongo in that moment in time in my parent's home. I'm the one who chose the movie. I'm the one to suggest the movie. I'm the one who turned it on and should have known better. I was a bad Pongo.

Pongo's job is not to determine if my mother should be offended or not. Pongo's job is to never offend my mother -- along with every single individual user everywhere in the world, regardless of their personal and community mores.

Thus, a user will determine offensive content in advance, such that Pongo never offends.

In my mother's house while watching Pongo, that tremendously popular Hollywood blockbuster would never be available to watch. It wouldn't show up as an option in my house, because Pongo would know it offends my mother.

I use many various digital, streaming and social media services. I know how y'all do things. It's not working. Nobody has created a system which takes care of the individual needs of a user. I know, I've tried. Nobody is actually looking after my mother.

One service I use allows me to utilize a Hollywood rating system to curtail content, conceivably for child viewing. When I selected nothing above a PG rating to get rid of swear words, all Fox News broadcasts disappeared. Don't laugh. All CBS News broadcasts disappeared too. I couldn't watch the news or most anything else. My options for viewing went down to near nill. My household was allowed to watch silly children's cartoons, and I couldn't edit out the cartoons which actually were offensive.

Our current solutions are silly. They don't address real life concerns in a digital age.

It's 2021, folks. We have the most brilliant minds in the world creating amazing artificial intelligence systems. We can create a system to individually address the personal needs of every single user, everywhere in the world. Pongo will do just that.

#GoPongo

A Paid Happily, Highly Monetized Contract

Pongo will contract with the biggest corporate users, down to a personal individual user, to highly monetize their content in a happy manner.

Pongo takes that paid contract seriously. We are literally receiving a cash payment every month to fulfill our end of the deal.

I don't care if it's only $2 per month. It's not the amount paid for the services, it's the fact that a customer paid for that service and is expecting a powerful, contracted result.

Some of our customers paying us for these services are the biggest content generators in the world. Their content is worth more than I've ever seen in my lifetime. Their content is worth more than most businesses in the world.

Some of the individual events -- the Super Bowl -- have an entire annual business for a bunch of massive corporations with powerful wealthy shareholders wrapped up in one singular event. That event is for all the marbles for the entire year for that business.

And Pongo is paid $2 per month to bring that business more cash from that event than they could earn doing that event in their current provable business solution and systems.

That responsibility isn't lost on me. It's definitely not misunderstood by Pongo.

For an individual user, that same weight applies. Every person cares deeply about their content. It's personal to them. Pongo will recognize the importance of that personal responsibility we owe each user.

Because of this, our paid $2 per month contract carries with it overwhelming responsibility.

Pongo's moral and ethical responsibility is to do everything within my power to make sure users' content and their businesses succeed because of Pongo.

Pongo Bank

Additionally, the same holds for Pongo's need to quickly create a literal bank.

I have chosen Mechanics Bank, headquartered down in the Silicon Valley area, to be the mentor bank as part of the Pongo Launch Engine. Pongo Bank won't be under or a subsidiary of Mechanics Bank. Pongo will be its own separate banking institution.

Everyone's Real -- No Fake Accounts and Bots

Pongo will know everyone's identity. Some may choose to be anonymous or have an AKA as their Pongo handle, allowing the public to wonder who is making all that money. Pongo will know everybody. There will be no fake accounts and bots. Pongo is a bank.

Sinister activity will drop to near nill when everyone is known by Pongo.

The day of the dreaded bots is over once Pongo is launched.

There's a value to charging $2 per month for a contract.

26

Some Additional Applications Served by the Pongo Launch Engine

Remember how I said that unlike other tech companies and applications, Pongo isn't a one dimensional Engine?

Let me give you a peek at some of the other applications which will be served by our simple, basic, comprehensive multidimensional Pongo Launch Engine.

Online Education

One of the most powerful additional applications of the Pongo Engine is its ability to handle online education. Online learning is native to Pongo. It's as if Pongo was created for it.

When I first started sharing this concept over a decade ago, nobody could conceive of 2020. Lo and behold, we needed Pongo last year.

Pongo is built for online education.

First, Pongo is super-duper secure and safe.

Second, online education doesn't just involve an online video chat with a group of students. Pongo, at its core, already has all of the necessary tools a teacher needs, combined into one platform. An online school shouldn't need to hop out of the online video meeting to go to a different application to deal with submission of written homework assignments, messaging, etc. This is all done in the native application of

Pongo. The system was created for that all to happen at once. All aspects of online education will be already created by Pongo. It's a matter of using Pongo for an additional purpose.

Third, Pongo opens up the ability for an online educational system to reach beyond the borders of the brick and mortar school. Using the Pongo systems already created for news delivery and interaction with live events, an online school can reach out to serve students across a state or around the world.

Fourth, Pongo could create an additional, lucrative income stream for a brick and mortar school, just by doing what Pongo was built to do.

We needed Pongo in 2020. We need to build Pongo now.

Internet Radio

In its native form, Pongo automatically handles all music use licensing and pays out royalties for music makers using the Pongo PayOut System.

Even if a song is playing in the background of a stadium or while viewing online, Pongo recognizes the music and calculates royalties based on the amount of cash flowing through the Pongo Engine while the song is playing.

Musicians and their licensing agents would prefer to have their music playing on Pongo, because Pongo will finally give the musicians and owners of the intellectual property their rightful royalties instantly and automatically. They will make far more cash from Pongo in royalties than they would make in the old, traditional brick and mortar music licensing methods.

Rather than cutting off and deleting videos and live events, based on music licensing issues, as is currently happening, Pongo PayOut will deposit in the music makers account a large amount of cash. Right now, musicians and their labels aren't making money because someone happened to buy a box of Tide or a Ford truck while their song was playing in the background.

With the Pongo Engine, automatically, a person could launch an internet radio station on a local level with $2 per month and have all the music available for them to play, all the while automatically taking care of all licensing issues.

It's all digital. It's 2021. We can do this. It's easy.

So many local radio stations are gone. We can fix that too.

Political Fundraising and Live Rallies

All of the pieces and parts in Pongo are ideal to fully handle all aspects of an online political campaign, including fundraising and bringing live political events to the masses.

Yes, every politician in 2020 needed Pongo to be running. It would have changed the dynamics of races, especially on a local level. So many times this last year as I watched a political speech, online rally or digital political event, I thought about the desperate need for Pongo's Engine, especially when it came to harnessing fundraising power with a political movement.

Churches and Religious Institutions

All of the sudden, even the smallest churches, had to go digital in 2020. Many will likely continue their online worship services and digital connection with their congregations.

Many struggled, dealing with competing alternate digital platforms, to make 2020 work for these religious institutions. Pastors with a congregation of 20 had to become digital experts to provide their spiritual services. Smoogle-Boogle's TubeyTV and Bluebookey-Facey Thing primarily handled many of the aspects -- not expertly, I must add.

When one thinks of the overall capabilities of Pongo, my system would have worked brilliantly, as if it were created for such. Pongo would even help a church handle receiving their tithes and offerings.

My Personal Invitation

Dr. John Chesnut, Wycliffe Bible Translators and **Tim Neu,** Wycliffe Associates

Rupert Murdoch, News Corp and Fox Corporation

Hans Vestberg, Verizon Communications

Larry Ellison, Oracle Corporation

Robert Mark Bakish, ViacomCBS

Elon Musk, SpaceX and Tesla, Inc.

James D. Farley Jr., Ford Motor Company

David Scott Taylor, Procter & Gamble

William Rodney McMullen, Kroger

Sir Tim Berners-Lee, Inrupt

Jack Dorsey, Twitter

Robert A. Kotick, Activision Blizzard

Roger Goodell, National Football League

Dr. Patrick Soon-Shiong, Los Angeles Times and Nant Capital

David D. Smith, Sinclair Broadcast Group

Charles "Charlie" C. Hale, Hale Global and Patch

John DeCero, Mechanics Bank

Michael Hallén, Vizrt Group (NewTek)

Plus, Three Currently Empty Positions

This entire book has been written specifically for you. I want to personally invite you and your family of companies to join me as a member of the Founding 21 Pongo Launch Engine.

I own the provisional patent pending for the business systems and processes of the Pongo Engine. I would be honored to exclusively share with your company these details upon receiving a signed written nondisclosure agreement and meeting to discuss the matter further.

Three of the 21 slots are empty. I am reserving those three slots for families of technology which likely will be identified in our first meeting as possible companies needed to complete the full Pongo Launch Engine.

I am hopeful that we all can get together in one place, at one time to all make a decision to commit to explore the possibility of bringing Pongo to life.

I had hoped we could do such at a watering hole in my hometown, in the shadow of Mount Shasta, in Northern California. There are plenty of fields around town to land your helicopter. We're used to this around here. I want you to see and envision how small we have to go to build an Engine which works financially, even in a small town such as mine. You could easily slip in and out of town without the world knowing. Plus, it's a gorgeous setting you may have never seen before.

In light of current personal meeting conditions, of course we all could meet online. Does anyone have a truly safe platform for us to meet, considering Pongo hasn't been launched yet to bring that to the world?

If you know someone else on my list, would you please consider throwing Pongo a bone and helping me bring us all together?

I look forward to the possibility of speaking with you further about launching Pongo and the role your family of companies could play in this unique opportunity.

Respectfully submitted,

Daniel Webster
Pongo's Parent

Index of Companies and Names

Twitter, @Jack, Jack Dorsey Edition Notice, Chapters 3, 9, 15, 23, My Personal Invitation

Verizon Communications, Hans Vestberg Edition Notice, Chapters 5, 9, 16, 18, 19, 22, My Personal Invitation

ViacomCBS, CBS, WCBS, Paramount, MaxPreps Sports, Robert Mark Bakish Edition Notice, Chapters 5, 12, 13, 14, 17, 18, 22, 25, My Personal Invitation

Vizrt Group, NewTek, Michael Hallén Edition Notice, Chapters 5, My Personal Invitation

Walmart, "MartInWalls" Edition Notice, Chapter 23

Wycliffe Bible Translators, Dr. John Chesnut and Wycliffe Associates, Tim Neu Edition Notice, Chapters 2, 13, 19, My Personal Invitation

YouTube TV, "TubeyTV" Edition Notice, Chapters 5, 26

About Daniel Webster

Mr. Daniel Webster is solutions oriented. He finds solutions for problems.

Daniel Webster received his Juris Doctor from Western State University College of Law, where he served as president of the Student Bar Association. He earned the American Jurisprudence Award for Contracts, California Property Law, Torts, Constitutional Law, Professional and Moral Responsibility and Legal Writing. He was inducted into the Peter M Elliott American Inn of Court.

In the mid-1980s, Mr. Webster was chosen to launch one of Apple Computer's first ten university bookstore test locations at Biola University to sell their new Macintosh. It was a success for the new tech company. Mr. Webster sold the original Apple Macintosh model and had a pre-Mac Lisa on his desk as well.

Mr. Webster was part of the initial sales team for Prodigy, while a corporate account executive for Sears Business Systems, one of Prodigy's founding companies. He also achieved corporate sales success in the formative years of the personal computer industry at Inacomp Computers.

Daniel Webster has always been solutions oriented, coming up with results-based projects to bring about the necessary marketing and technology impacts for his large corporate clients, such as Hughes Corporation, RAND Corporation, TRW, ARCO, Hilton and DirecTV. He was ranked as the top grossing computer sales representative in the Western United States.

Prior to purchasing his local weekly adjudicated newspaper, Mr. Webster served as the interim editor of the Siskiyou Daily News, in Yreka, Calif. He was the owner, editor and publisher of the Pioneer Press, Butte Valley Star and Klamath Courier in Northern California and Southern Oregon. He currently publishes Scott Valley News, Yreka News, Siskiyou News, Mount Shasta News and other regional news sites on Facebook, where he has a following of 81 percent of his county's population. His current news service is a labor of love for his community, after its loss of their local newspapers.

He served as president of his Student Body Association at his alma mater Etna High School, in Etna, Calif. Mr. Webster did undergraduate work at Biola University, in La Mirada, Calif., with majors in Business Administration, Systems Analysis and Bible, as well as DeVry Institute of Technology, in Phoenix, Ariz., majoring in Systems Analysis.

Mr. Webster lives on a small farm, near his hometown with a population of 800, in the shadow of Mt. Shasta.

Daniel Webster is Pongo's Parent. He is currently seeking to launch Pongo, the World's Largest Communications Network Connecting Every Device for Every Person in Every Language Everywhere on Earth, to save the news industry and the internet. Daniel Webster is the author of the book #GoPongo.

www.ingramcontent.com/pod-product-compliance
Lightning Source LLC
LaVergne TN
LVHW012200040326
832903LV00003B/35